The Unsinkable Bambi Lake

also from Bambi Lake

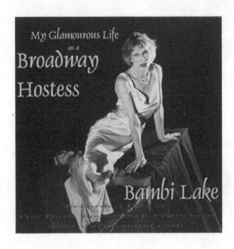

The Unsinkable Bambi Lake

A Fairy Tale Containing the Dish
on Cockettes, Punks, and Angels

Introduction by
Exene Cervenka

Bambi Lake
with Alvin Orloff

Manic D Press
San Francisco

Cover photograph by Daniel Nicoletta
Additional photo acknowledgments on page 157

Library of Congress Cataloging-in Publication Data

Lake, Bambi, 1950-
 The unsinkable Bambi Lake : a fairy tale containing the dish on cockettes, punks, and angels / Bambi Lake with Alvin Orloff; introduction by Exene Cervenka.
 p. cm.
ISBN 978-1-945665-02-8 (pbk.)(2nd edition)
1. Lake, Bambi, 1950-   . 2. Transsexuals—United States--Biography. 3. Transsexualism—United States—Case studies.
I. Orloff, Alvin, 1961-   .11.Title.
HQ77.8.L34A3 1996 305.3—dc20
[B]   96-10093
CIP

Dedicated to
Kevin Purcell
and
Michael Collins
a.k.a. Diet Popstitute

CONTENTS

CONTENTS

A fairy tale of a time before Ronald Reagan. Tell me a story. Before 1984. Tell me stories about San Francisco punk rock and the Summer of Love and she-male force. Before regular normal people like yuppies and rich kids discovered thrift stores and the FREE glamour and MAGIC to be gotten there. That's what saved us from having to sell out to THEM. Bambi got to be an Angel of Light. She got to do it all first. She gets to be outrageous. She gets to live underground, in the cultural bombshelter that's helped us (artists, punks, queers, sexworkers, writers, outcasts, losers, whoever ain't into their normal thing) survive the '60s, '70s, '80s, '90s. We will survive the millennium. Bambi's fairy tale is true. Her life has been a protest march in high heels. YOU should live a more interesting life after you finish this book. Maybe we can learn transgender kindness. Fairy tale appreciation. Even for the sailors...

Exene Cervenka
Los Angeles, California

Johnny Purcell, age 8

Up the Airy Mountain

I've been up all night thinking about an elves and fairies book I got at the Convent of the Sacred Heart kindergarten.

> *Up the Airy Mountain*
> *Down the Rushy Glen*
> *We Dare Not Go A-huntin'*
> *For Fear of Little Men*

Or something like that. I loved the gorgeous illustrations of fairies dancing around an oak tree under the moon. When I was little, the best present I ever got was a pink styrofoam glittered fairy house which just tweaked me out of my mind forever. My parents gave it to me. It was like, "Okay, you're a little drag queen." The present was not only beautiful but sort of prophetic because my life has been something of a fairy tale.

I was born John Joseph Purcell on October 20, 1950 on the Libra/Scorpio cusp — the same birth date as Arthur Rimbaud and Sarah Bernhardt, giving me strong ties to Belle Époque Paris. I was the fourth of eight kids in a totally Irish Catholic family. Our surname is Purcell but my mother's maiden name is Mulcahy, and my grandmother was a Brophy. It doesn't get any greener than that. My parents were married at the poetically named Our Lady of the Wayside church near our hometown of Woodside, California, just south of San Francisco. It's a quaint idyllic town with a little red schoolhouse and a country store dating from the 1880s. Were you to come visit us, you'd turn off Woodside Road at a little bar called the Peanut Farm (love that name) and go down a winding road into a hollow, poetically named Woodside Glens. There you'd see our little house, tended to by our pit bull terrier, Bully. You'd find us little moppets peering at you with our huge liquid eyes from a giant oak tree that overhung the road in which we'd sit for hours.

Woodside is very affluent and my father worked as a carpenter and landscaper on the Galvin estate. He did well enough for himself that he could spoil my mother with lots of hats and a live-in housemaid. The whole place was positively enchanted, like Sleeping Beauty's house. When the Galvins were deported back to Ireland for tax evasion we had to move to Redwood City and more modest circumstances.

I had little in common with either my parents or my siblings. I was the artistic one, expressing a rather striking, perhaps even shocking, flare for the feminine arts of dress-up and make-believe. I was fascinated by dolls, plays, puppets, dance, and music. I used to listen to the hit parade hosted by Gisele MacKenzie, and when the song from the Moulin Rouge came on I would spontaneously begin doing interpretive dancing complete with graceful floorwork and back bends. My grandmother, who lived with us, made little wings for me out of newspaper and wildflowers in which I would flit about the yard. Despite that indulgence she would sometimes giggle at my feminine excesses. My father firmly reprimanded her for that saying, "Stella, don't ever laugh at that boy." He'd been raised in San Francisco near Finocchio's when it was on Polk Street back in the late 1930s, and knew what gay people were.

When I was very young I would sleep in my parents' bed, and as I was drifting off I would often see little dots of multicolored light come into the room, and they would dance me to sleep. I think my mother favored my older brothers but my father favored me. I had a certain strange sensuality as a child and there was an attraction on my part for him that I think he felt and reciprocated. Lying in my father's arms at night I vividly recall dreaming that I was a royal child in a Cecil B. DeMille-style Egyptian or Babylonian court with handsome scantily clad servants kneeling and fanning me with giant palm fronds. I had a recurring dream until I was about seven that I was being held by a blue man, sort of a pagan angelic spirit. I used to believe this man was my guardian angel but now I think he was my unconscious mind's vision of my extremely handsome father, who looked like the very young, very Irish, matinee idol John Wayne.

The rest of the world was not as understanding as my father. One day I was in the backyard trying on some gowns I had collected from the neighborhood girls when a realtor who was inspecting our house told my mother that there was a little girl with a crewcut playing in the backyard. I was always mortifying my mother. Needless to say there were some problems with school. While I loved art class, I hated anything like American Government or Algebra. I'd get A's in the former and D's in the latter. I needed smart drugs but they hadn't been invented yet. Phys Ed was a bit of a trial, too. Maybe if I'd started drinking coffee at the age of eight, I could have been aggressive enough to play flag ball, but as it was I just didn't have the energy for that sort of thing.

All through elementary school I believed in fairies. My best friend, David, who was an altar boy at my church and very smart, encouraged me. He said they were all around him and he could give me one but I wouldn't be able to see it because it was invisible. He claimed he went to Fairyland every night and promised to take me along. I'd fall asleep every night waiting for him to come with his entourage of fairies. Then I'd dream of going there, walking through the jeweled tunnel (Freudian?) just as he'd described it. The next day we'd act as if we'd actually gone. David was related to Russ Tamblyn, the gorgeous actor and dancer, and David always said we'd go to Hollywood to meet him and he'd give us screen tests. In third grade, long before I was exhibiting blatantly feminine characteristics, David told me I had more female hormones than male hormones. He knew stuff like that because he had not only the Invisible Man (a see-through plastic biology toy) but also the Invisible Woman. He was really rather fabulous.

David lived with his mother who, along with her handsome boyfriend, would take David and me to see musicals at the drive-in while they made out in the back seat. His mother also went to the theater every week to see a new musical like *Pal Joey*, *Porgy and Bess*, or *Kiss Me Kate*. Later she'd show us the program, play us the album, and tell us the story. One Halloween she dressed David up as Sir Francis Drake, all in velvet, and put me (as did my own mother on more than one Halloween) in full drag. She put her hat on my head and stuffed cotton balls around the inside rim to create a fabulous platinum blonde wig. I click-clopped down the sidewalk all night in her petticoats, high heels, and red lipstick. She said when I grew up I would work at Finocchio's, the notorious female impersonator club in San Francisco that she frequented. Every week in the *Redwood City Tribune* they'd have a new ad with their featured performer. They'd have teasingly androgynous names like "Mr." Bobby Monroe, or

"Mr." Tracy Dare, and would work fierce 1940s B-movie star looks, like Yvonne De Carlo. David's mother was rather fabulous, too.

One day a strange boy named Richard told me an old abandoned house near school was full of Sleeping Beauty furniture, with satin curtains, gowns of silk, and lace jewel boxes full of diamonds and emeralds, rubies, and pearls. I believed him firmly. I dreamed of becoming a fairy princess, and the abandoned house full of finery was just what I needed. He said the house was under a wicked spell so only he could go in. I forced him to let me watch him enter and he came running out with an old box of sugar. I began to cry hysterically and walked back to school. The principal, Mr. Hutchinson, saw me and asked me to explain my problem. I told him everything. He knelt down close to me and said, "Johnny, there are no fairies."

I sobbed, "Yes, there are! Yes, there are!" Eventually I calmed down and walked home disillusioned.

Musicals became my replacement for Fairyland. David and his mother felt a little responsible for having encouraged me in my fairy fantasies and were very nice, bringing me even more fabulous musical soundtrack albums to listen to. There were also the annual TV productions of Rodgers and Hammerstein's *Cinderella*, and Mary Martin's *Peter Pan* to look forward to, and of course *The Wizard of Oz*. When I was twelve, the summer before I started high school, I became eligible for the Music Drama Workshop, a summer program run jointly by three local public schools. I worked my way up to being head set designer while also getting lead roles. I lived for our summer musicals: *My Fair Lady, Carousel, The Music Man, Camelot*. We did a production of *Brigadoon* with all the sexy surfer boys in kilts and the girls done up like wenches. I'll never forget the sight of all the mod surfer girls from Woodside gliding into the parking lot on their bicycles with their long hair flowing on hot summer mornings. Steffanie Anna, the star, sticks out particularly in my mind. She was Icelandic and had black silky hair halfway to her knees and white, white skin. She wore a purple cotton babydoll dress with lime green fishnets and was always painting her shoes different colors. We worshiped her. Later on, she appeared on *The Dating Game*, and I'm not sure, but I heard she became the voice of Smurfette and made a fortune.

I survived high school by plunging myself into the never-ending whirl of local theater. We were always doing shows, and going to wild all-night parties at the beach or at my friend Kenny's house. Despite this freewheeling environment, I had to sneak away after school to ballet class. To have been discovered would have meant total shame; that was how you became totally queer in the '60s, studying ballet. Kenny, my classmate, took the plunge and ended up dating Jerry H., and his apartment was used as the set for the movie *The Gay Deceivers*. He was pretty "out" even in school, like he'd insist he was going to play Dolly Levi, the Carol Channing role, in *Hello, Dolly*.

Luckily for me, I grew up in Redwood City right near the Circle Star Theater in San Carlos. It soon became my second home. I acted in children's productions of *Babes in Toyland*, *Cinderella*, and *Heidi*. I also worked as a stagehand for the adult productions that offered me the grandest experience I could hope for, working with real actors from Broadway and Hollywood.

The chorus girls and boys — the gypsies — were really something, pure glamour. They were all from Hollywood, beautiful, talented, and sexy. The girls dressed like Ann-Margret or Elke Sommer: stretchpants, cha-cha boots, fur coats, scarves, and sunglasses. They had great names like Michelle Abelle and Julie Genet. I think Teri Garr worked there, too. They drove sports cars! A lot of the chorus boys were probably queer. That to me is the ideal gay boy, a theater queen with a cute little body, a baby face, who actually tap dances. To me that's erotic almost. One boy, Sean, looked like Ryan O'Neal and the other boys would give him a hard time saying, "Oh, Sean, you're so butch." They would have cocktail parties in motor lodges and show us younger kids the pictures (like of drunk boys putting on wigs) later. One actor from the New York cast of *Oliver* was really hot for us young stagehands and nailed my best friend Bill, who was junior high school president.

Over the years I got to meet people like the opera star Patrice Munsel, Jack Benny, Ricky Nelson, and Gisele MacKenzie, the hostess of my favorite radio hit parade show and singer. I met the original Miss Mazeppa from *Gypsy* and sold her my papier-mâché jewelry. Papier-mâché jewelry was a big home crafts fad in the '60s. We'd make earrings or bracelets from paste and paper, paint them day-glo colors outlined with Pentel magic markers, then shellac them. They inevitably fell apart rather quickly. My friend Kenny helped me get a role in the chorus of *Oliver*, and Davy Jones came to visit us. Davy Jones was the English member of The Monkees, the rock band created to star in that wildly popular weekly TV series. He wore a Carnaby Street captain's hat, and had lovely white skin, dark eyes, and very red cheeks. Sigh! The ultimate was Georgia Brown from *Oliver* in her teased-up big black hair, red dress, purple cotton slips, high button shoes, smoking a cigar, belting out "As Long As He Needs Me" every night for three weeks. She was rumored to be a heroin addict (legally in London) and she stayed on a houseboat in Sausalito. She would arrive at the theater in an old Jaguar wearing a mod tweed pantsuit with flared cuffs, a turtleneck sweater with a large gold medallion, and spike heel boots. What a goddess.

Redwood City is sort of like Peyton Place with all the rich people on one side of the tracks and all of us on the other. In my neighborhood Latins ruled. I had all these hot Latino neighbors. In one family nearby, the oldest boy Jim won the Pony Contest at the Rec Center. He always wore skintight white or black Levi's revealing every gorgeous curve of his huge box. I always wonder what the nuns at catechism thought. Down the street was another family with hot Latino sons. Bill, the oldest, was the heartthrob of town, and

Sunday (Domingo), the youngest, was my first big crush. He wore pointed loafers with the little fringe leather knots dangling on them when he was eight. Sexy at eight. I went to his Little League games and watched him pitch. He was always nice to me. Their sister, Terri, taught me to do the Mashed Potato at Sally Soul's house. Sally Soul (her real name) kissed one of the Righteous Brothers at her senior prom!

In a lot of ways growing up in Redwood City was a lot like the book (and later the movie) *The Outsiders*, with warring gangs. There was a rumble every year between the seniors and juniors at my school (Sequoia High), the object of which was to capture a beat-up kerosene lamp. This rivalry has been going on since the 1920s, and it was a serious manhood ritual. Call it macho, but to me it was as natural as the weather, like young elk bucking antlers on Mutual of Omaha's *Wild Kingdom*. Despite my obvious lack of masculinity, I was protected in this world because I came from a big family with lots of brothers. I'd go to school every day with my older brother Jim (who looked like Marky Mark) in his friend Rick's canary yellow '56 Chevy (raised in the back with a black leather Tijuana tuck and roll interior). He'd gun it to 90 mph, and screech to a halt before gliding into the parking lot.

THE GODS OF REDWOOD CITY

Everyone was making out but me
Parking in the hills on Saturday nights
Back in the '60s in Redwood City
Up by the Cross looking out at the lights
I was odd and thin and didn't fit in
I left and never went back
But now I'm starting to long for La Honda
And something I lack

After the Gold Rush they found a new kind of gold
That they could harvest up at the river or down in Mexico
The boys I grew up with, beautiful and bad
Became buccaneers on the seven seas
Pirates in green plaid
Mod hippie surfers
With high cheekbones
Crazy hawk eyes
Lazy baritones
Tall as the redwood trees
Were the Gods of Redwood City

We all moved to La Honda
Or the Emerald Lake
Lived in little cabins with wild roses
Under Maxfield Parrish blue skies
At daybreak
Looking for mysteries beneath the shroud
On the beach at San Gregorio
I saw visions of lovers in slow moving clouds
Naked and holy as Michelangelo
They got into John Mayall
I got into Jerry Hall
They got into music and drugs
I got into drag and thugs
Up at the Cross, up at Handley Rock
They'd talk about the lamp fight
Drinking beer between big hits of pot
I'm starting to call them into a ring
Like enchanted dogs they will come when I sing
My siren song for the Gods of Redwood City

Unlike all the other queens I've met in my life, I don't have too many horror stories about P.E. I did worry about not looking good next to the other boys. We were forced to walk naked from the locker to the showers. I was embarrassed by my dick size because I had one of those dicks that hangs small when it's soft. Getting a boner in the shower was out of the question in 1964, so that wasn't even an issue. I just wanted to measure up. Later on, around age sixteen or so, I stopped feeling bad when, to my relief, my frequent boners became pretty darn large. I may not have been much to look at in the showers, but I was somethin' to see behind the barn.

Because I was a Purcell, the other guys were nice to me. I did have one rather sarcastic P.E. teacher however, who had dated my mother in the 1940s and would taunt me in front of the entire class saying, "How could such a beautiful woman give birth to such a lame duck of a son?" It wasn't always that bad though. The next year my P.E. teacher praised me in front of the class for some tumbling I'd done on stage in *Oliver*. I told him about my audition for *The Unsinkable Molly Brown* and he teased me by calling me Molly Brown. It all sounds trivial now but when you're a teenager it's a big deal how the coach treats you in front of the guys. I hate the way young gay boys are excluded, taught to hate their bodies, and made to feel inadequate if they're not good at competitive sports. Boys can cue in on who's queer and who's not at a very young age, and effeminate boys are ritualistically humiliated by being picked last for teams. Luckily, gorgeous, red headed, freckle-faced Rick Rider would pick me first for flag ball and help me get through the game.

I loved being a teenager in the '60s. I went to see the Dave Clark 5, and Sonny and Cher once. Sonny had on his shaggy coat and Cher was in velvet hiphugger bellbottoms with a fur-trimmed velvet hooded jacket. Cher gave this little child right near me a flower. Years later my friends and I would go to the Fillmore to see Janis Joplin,

Jimi Hendrix, and Jim Morrison. We'd do acid and the girls would get under the stage and listen to Janis stomp. We'd also go to Be-Ins at Golden Gate Park and buy pot on Haight Street, but in spite of all that counterculture stuff I still loved old theater and corny musicals best.

I never had long hair because I was always in shows doing Ibsen or Chekhov or something. It kind of wrecked me as far as being underground. I thought I'd grow up and work in sitcoms, like *McHale's Navy* or something. I would always be listening to Judy Garland albums with my friend Kevin, or watching Barbra Streisand specials. Teenagers didn't know about homosexuality in 1965, we just knew we loved JUDY. Fortunately nobody minded my being just a little bit naff. I was even best friends with the boy voted "Best Looking" in our senior class yearbook. I loved his name, Byron Woodside. He played football but read T.S. Eliot and Aldous Huxley's early romantic novels. Once my pals said, "Hey, Purcell! We saw a girl in A&W who looked just like you." And this one boy said real innocently, "You'd make a really good looking girl." He said it in a nice way.

I idolized the boys I grew up with. We were the golden boys of the late '60s. The boys of summer. The baby boom boys. Surfer boys. Madras. Baggies. Pendletons. Despite coming from a poor family I was always well dressed, too. I had shoplifting at the Tiger Shop in Hillsdale Mall down to an art. This was the height of postwar affluence and optimism, before teen angst became the norm. My older brother had a Woody (a four-door, wood-paneled 1940s stationwagon) and his long blonde-haired girlfriend, Barbra, won trophies for surfing in Santa Cruz. We were like something from an old beach party movie, *Beach Blanket Bingo*. I love their names, the aforementioned Rick and Byron, also Rudick, Kip, Butch, Buckey, and Dick. They sounded like '60s B-movie stars, or perhaps '70s Falcon video porn models. For me, these boys were the standard of male beauty and charm to which I hold everyone else. I found everything about them erotic, and was constantly about to burst with repressed sexual desire.

Johnny Purcell (on far right) with family & friends, age 18

Twinkle, Twinkle Little Star

After high school I started at Cañada Junior College, majoring in theater, naturally. One day I was hitchhiking to Menlo Park, where I was starring in a production of *The Boyfriend*, when a 1930s sedan coupe pulled up beside me, and the young man inside offered me a lift. I learned that he was a pianist, and he ended up accompanying me to rehearsal where he sat in with the band. After that, he would show up now and again, always driving a 1930s Cadillac or Lincoln. His name was Peter. He lived nearby, and had a house decorated entirely in Art Deco and hung with Maxfield Parrish prints. Even the telephones were period, and the phonograph was a Victrola! He gave me my first gay kiss.

One night he and his friends got me dressed up in his grandmother's green plaid taffeta evening gown with big ruffles and took me to San Francisco to the Palace Theater. There I saw Sylvester — yes, the same one who later went on to Disco Superstardom, but this was 1970 and he was only locally notorious — in a gorgeous '30s gown singing Connie Boswell's "Where Are You?" He was behind a gauze scrim with a little marbleized staircase and an airbrushed backdrop of a black bird with a camellia in its mouth, against a night sky. Peter accompanied him on piano.

Afterwards, at a glamorous party at Steven Arnold's Secret Cinema, I met some of Peter's friends, members of the hot inner circle of performers at the Palace who were called The Cockettes. They were all into '30s chic and drag. That night, Steven, who was a mentor to the Cockettes as well as a filmmaker and collector, was showing the silent film classic *Salome*. It starred Alla Nazimova, and everyone was very impressed that my great uncle, James Brophy, had acted with her.

Not long after we met, Peter began driving me up to the Palace so I could choreograph the Cockettes' new show, *Tinsel Tarts in a Hot Coma*. It was a lewd slinky LSD-influenced, film noir version of *42nd Street* that ended in a huge finale set to "Lullaby of Broadway." Like most Cockettes productions, the play ran for several weekends and was revived a few more times after its initial run. One night Joanna Carson, Lee Radziwill, Truman Capote, and Rex Reed were in the audience! I got to hang out at fabulous Cockettes parties, homes, and rehearsals. It was incredibly exciting for me.

By this time I had also discovered the joys of gay sex. There are certain moments one never forgets. I was going to see my girlfriend Kim, hitchhiking by the Whipple Avenue on-ramp to the Bayshore Freeway. A very handsome stranger in a suit with tight slacks driving a sports car pulled up and offered me a lift. Racing down the highway, he put his hand on my knee. I jumped, and he, quite a gentleman, pulled back. My entire body tensed, my throat went dry, time stood still, the engine roared. We were going eighty miles an hour. I reached over and grabbed his wrist, moving it over to my now eight-inch, hard-as-a-rock, eighteen-year-old boner. For a while he just held it there. Then he pulled down my zipper, freed and began stroking my dick which was now burning hot. I get physically hot during sex. Strange manly fingertips on me, his cool palm, up and down. It seemed to go on forever. I put my hand on his crotch and felt him hard. He veered off the freeway and began winding up into the San Mateo hills. I held onto the dashboard panting in ecstasy, getting ready to come. He reached for his handkerchief. I shot all over the place as he smoothly managed to catch my molten white hot cum in midair, protecting his precious luxe interior. I levitated. I felt weightless and happy. He invited me home but Catholic guilt was beginning to creep in, and I insisted he drop me off so I could meet Kim.

My first night of real lovemaking came not much later, when I was in a production of *St. George and The Dragon* at the very first Renaissance Pleasure Faire in San Rafael. The actors spent the nights at the fairground, and one warm summer evening around a blazing campfire and a full moon, to the sound of hypnotic flute and drum music, I saw a young man staring at me intently. I stared back and got a hard-on. He took me to his sleeping bag behind the main stage and I laid my nude body on top of his and humped him madly and shot all over his warm male hips and stomach. It was my first time and it was very, very beautiful! I also discovered The Stud, Polk Street, and older men: twenty-six-year-olds! This was the *Boys in the Band* era. Water beds. Plastic beaded curtains. I met the rather butch number who introduced me to sodomy (both ways!) at the old Patch Street Baths. He lived on upper Market Street and had a private art gallery. The day after our first night together I overheard him on the phone telling a compatriot that he had cried like a baby at a recent Charles Pierce farewell show. Meanwhile, I was still living at home with my mother, and things were getting tense. My parents had let me play with dolls and eventually even paid for my ballet lessons (I was, after all, their "Hollywood child") but when I came out to my mom that was going a bit too far. I told her on the way to the Oakland Induction Center. It was 1968, the height of the Vietnam War, and I had to stand in line in my underwear with all the other draft-age boys like lambs to the slaughter. I wrote on my clipboard in large bold letters: I'M GAY. My mother pretty much wrote me off after I told her. I moved to the Twin Oaks, a sort of sleazy hotel in San Francisco's Tenderloin. I was thrown out a week later for doing drag. Fortunately, one of the Cockettes, Hibiscus, was forming a new group called the Angels of Light, and had an opening at the house where they lived at Church and 17th Streets. So, at the tender age of twenty, I moved into what an alternative paper of the time called, "A hotbed of screaming faggotry." It was 1971 and graffitied on the side of the house was a slogan that has kind of stuck with me: Sisters, Rise Up!

Bambi with Moon Trent

Awake in a Dream

The Angels of Light house on Church Street was enchanted. It was decorated with all the sets from the shows they did: glittered cardboard swans, grapes, what have you. The people who lived there were all on welfare but, by living communally, could afford a huge flat in a Victorian haunted house with gables, big attic rooms, and bay windows. They said I could live there only if I went on welfare, so I went down to the Department of Social Services to apply for General Assistance. I needed a gimmick, so I stuck my thumb in my mouth and offered them a piece of paper which read *I must not speak / I must only seek / the truth of the fairy kingdom*. They asked me if I'd seen a psychiatrist. I just moved my lips without making a sound. Those were the days of real Academy Award performances for getting on welfare. People painted themselves gold, peed on the floor, covered themselves in mud and molasses. I'll never forget the great line, "I am the Brian. You are the moon. And everything is okay." There was a lot of LSD damage going around. I wouldn't fake my way onto welfare now but back then it seemed like the only way to survive.

The leader of the Angels was Hibiscus. He was a prophet and a visionary as well a great drag queen, performer, and director. Like me, he was a children's theater diva (he was cast in the Broadway musical production of *The Yearling* but got fired for muffing his lines) who'd become hopelessly queer. His whole family was theatrical: his mother was in the cult movie classic *The Honeymoon Killers*. In 1966, when he was sixteen, he ran away for a month to Hollywood, dyed his hair champagne pink, and sat in front of Grauman's Chinese Theater sipping pink champagne. He was sort of like Dennis the Menace in drag. In New York, he headed the children's theater program at La MaMa. He moved to San Francisco in '68, and years later I learned that he'd supposedly left New York under unusual circumstances. He'd been at a party having sex on acid with a beautiful boy on a bed by an open window. The boy rolled out and fell twenty stories to his death. The party broke up quickly and the next day Hibiscus was on his way to San Francisco.

At the Palace Theater in 1969, the dapper filmmaker/photographer Steven Arnold started showing midnight movies in a series called The Nocturnal Dream Show. The whole point was to smoke pot and trip out on these incredible films like early John Waters movies or the 1915 silent version of *The Wizard of Oz*. I used to go with my college friends and we'd get in by offering a joint to the ticket taker, a pretty boy with an Afro hairdo wearing full glitter makeup. The Cockettes sort of started by spontaneous combustion. Hibiscus and his friends would get up on stage in high fantasy drag, and sing and do stupid skits for the very stoned audience. This evolved into actual scripted theme shows, the first of which was called *Hollywood Babylon*, in which he played Jayne Mansfield while wearing beach balls for breasts. At the 1969 Halloween show he threw a bloody animal heart into the audience while singing "Piece of My Heart" and Janis Joplin was actually there!

Underneath the drag, Hibiscus was a very handsome blond young man with chiseled good looks softened by full, sensual lips. He had a nice round butt and when Janis Joplin saw him, she sent him a note backstage that said, "Nice show, Biscuits." He also had a big dick which made everyone like him all the more, and which came in handy later on when he became a call boy. He was on SSI because he had cancer in his legs, and he walked with a slight limp. He knew his life would be short, and his life was all about celebration.

Hibiscus's show drag consisted of whiteface with layers of colored rhinestones encircling his eyes. He would paint his lips with his fingers using tiny pots of thick crimson rouge. He wore a beard that he would encrust with glitter, creating the first genderfuck look. Widely imitated, never equaled. He'd frequently wear a shredded, ruffled, brightly colored Mardi Gras dress. Have I mentioned that Hibiscus was originally from Florida? He retained his full-on Southern Belle temperament. He was the sort of person who'd use his SSI check to buy ten bags of glitter and two expensive beaded vintage gowns at secondhand stores and then rip the gowns to shreds on stage. Now the crowning glory: Hibiscus always wore a headdress, often made of hibiscus-colored crepe paper flowers, calla lilies, and ostrich feathers. This passion for headdresses grew to the point where such things as gold glittered Viennese castles and glittered star-like Sputniks were used. Years later, *Beach Blanket Babylon*, the long-running cabaret show featuring impossibly large hats, was started as a tired, middle-aged, old school, non-drag, not funny, oh so tongue-in-cheek version of this. Once Hibiscus made a giant peacock fan which, when opened, was so large that as he walked downstage it bowled over a whole line of us dressed as Hindu

Kathakali dancers.

This is how the Angels of Light got started. The Cockettes did a show called *Tropical Heatwave Hot Voo Doo*, in which a drunken Hibiscus sang ten show tunes in a row. This precipitated a fight with Bobbi Venus, one of the other Cockettes, during which Hibiscus was thrown down a flight of stairs at the Grove Street Gay Center. After that incident Hibiscus left to start his own group, the Angels of Light, with a couple of other Cockettes and some street kids. They were urchins, gamins, enfants terribles, lost boys and fairy girls. A lot of them had graduated from prestigious arts colleges. The first Angels show in 1970 was at Grace Cathedral at Midnight Mass on Christmas Eve, and the Archbishop was there. Hibiscus dressed up as the Virgin Mary holding a naked baby surrounded by his drag disciples. Next he was filmed at Land's End beach as Christ on the cross being crucified by the Angels on Easter Sunday. All the early shows were performed at midnight on full moons for free, and unlike the Cockettes who wore old drag and sang '30s-style show tunes (what Hibiscus referred to as "mold"), the Angels' shows featured original songs and drag creations.

I had seen Hibiscus at the Palace so I knew who he was when I spotted him at The Grubstake, a restaurant hangout on Polk Street. He looked like a real sexy hippie beach boy but when he opened his mouth the voice of Jayne Mansfield came out. I was a bit taken aback. He told me he'd left the Cockettes and was starting his own group. He invited me to be in his upcoming show, having heard about my choreographing *Tinsel Tarts*. I didn't get to do it though because I inadvertently started dating his boyfriend, Miguel, a fiery, swarthy, Cuban queen-fucker. Hibiscus saw us together at rehearsal and afterwards when we were alone, calmly said to me, "I see you've met Miguel, how nice. I hope you enjoy it because you may not live long." He was dressed up in eighteenth century garb that day, and as he made his threat he put on a scary feathered jeweled mask. I was terrified and called the police who thought I was crazy. I ended up skipping the whole show, which turned out to be a real tragedy. It was at the legendary Grove Street Gay Center and it turned into an all-night psychedelic orgy. Allen Ginsberg sang his William Blake songs and the Angels dressed him up like an old Jewish mother in a housecoat and painted a huge third eye on his forehead. Not long after that, Miguel was flown off to appear in the movie *Holy Mountain* by Alejandro Jodorowsky, and with him out of the picture Hibiscus and I made up. Soon after I was asked to move into the Angels house.

The Angels house was a bit chaotic. The first night I moved in everybody got really, really drunk. I learned the meaning of the phrase "Rage Queen" as they screamed and carried on like maniacs. Fortunately that was a pretty rare occurrence, though you never knew when someone would just go off. There was a lot of random madness. People would be jumping on couches all the time. You'd see Hibiscus's famous drunken imitation of Jayne Mansfield getting fucked by a thousand men. Food fights, or even throwing up your food at the table, were common. We took down a wall once and didn't get around to cleaning up the rubble for months. Tahara put up a sign that read: This is not here — Yoko Oh No.

The thing that reminds me most of queer households today in its sick and twisted humor was when Ruby hung a mannequin torso labeled "Sharon Tate" with a knife in it in the dining room. It was a leftover prop from a Halloween show. I look back on it fondly now but at the time it sort of scared me. I was, as Hibiscus always said, like Katherine Hepburn from *Stage Door* — the reserved, classy, slender, talented one. Ruby saw my shocked expression when I saw the mannequin, and said nonchalantly, "Well, it happened." This wasn't some hippie dippy commune; these were twisted sisters. But we all loved each other.

We were very serious about our work. "Perfect your art" was our motto. The Angels were multicultural long before it was fashionable, incorporating Indian Hindu dancing, Japanese kabuki, Chinese opera, belly dancing, Balinese dance, Christmas fairy tales, Bible stories, Greek myths, Scheherazade, Nijinsky, Cocteau, Tennessee Williams, Von Sternberg films, Dietrich, Edith Piaf, Isadora Duncan, and Broadway musicals, often all in the same show. We were influenced a lot by Josephine Baker and Yma Sumac, and we all wanted to live in Europe. We loved the exotic, and the shows were always full of people playing enchanted animals and deities.

We'd eat big vegetarian meals prepared by Beaver and Rodney. Beaver was a cute blonde girl with a heart of pure gold who never wore shoes except in shows. She had an intense relationship with her dog, Saskia. To her everything was a pip, a word she used to describe something outrageous or ridiculously funny. She had genius-like artistic ability and a radiant stage presence. Today she is a top theater designer. She loved Rodney who loved Brian, whose baby she ended up having in a natural childbirth right at the house attended by all us drag queens. She screamed all night. She named her son Shom Shiel, which is out of the Bible and means "angel at the break of day." For the next few years we raised him and he appeared in shows with us. It was all quite lovely, and today Shom is a strikingly handsome and well-adjusted young man about town. Beaver's parents warned her in a letter that the child would be "chained to the subculture." We were all so thrilled. We wrote a show about it that took place on a pirate ship called the S.S. Subculture, and Beaver played the masthead and she sang this little ditty:

> *I am the masthead on this ship*
> *I think these pirates are a bunch of pips*
> *I can't wait to be set free*
> *they are all too queer for me*

Beaver was always shopping at the Salvation Army and coming home with fabulous finds that she had just "swooped," pieces of shiny material or animal print fabric that she used to create elaborate little appliqués. Once she created an outer space poodle with little pillows and she wrote a song to go with it: *I'm an oodle of a poodle who wants to noodle your caboodle till you doodle.* The sight of Beaver simulating oral sex with a drag queen and a banana at San Francisco State University precipitated a riot. It was at a Gay Lib party. Some women who apparently didn't realize she was a real girl felt she was demeaning womanhood or something and rushed the stage. Hibiscus shrieked, "Help! I'm being attacked by lesbians!" In the Angels' show *Holy Cow*, there was a breathtaking moment when Beaver, dressed as an Indian princess, crouched down, removed her veil, and transformed herself into a unicorn with hooves and horn. Amazing! She was Wendy to Hibiscus's Peter Pan, and we were the Lost Boys. The Angels were some of the most flamboyant characters I have ever come across.

The first time I saw Rodney he was standing under a poster designed by Hibiscus at a popular bar called The Stud. It read: "The Angels of Light need singers, dancers, actors, drag queens," accompanied by a glittered picture of Marlene Dietrich from *Blonde Venus*. Rodney had heavy makeup, long dirty hair and a short beard, muscular arms, and was dressed in trailing shredded taffeta and tulle. The next time I saw him, his hair was washed, and he was in a t-shirt and jeans. Then I realized that he was absolutely gorgeous, with beautiful Italian features and a muscular, voluptuous body. Like Hibiscus, he was a case study in androgyny. People were hypnotized by him, and his hippie-god drag was legendary. I'll never forget the sight of him one Thanksgiving morning, cooking at the stove in a tousled brown wig, wearing a torn cocktail dress and heels. When I told him he looked like Sophia Loren in *Two Women*, he told me he was doing his mother.

Tahara Nugi Whitewoman was named by Hibiscus after a character in a Charles Ludlam play. Ludlam was a campy, openly gay, Off Off Broadway avant-garde theater pioneer with whom Hibiscus had worked back in New York. His work was similar to ours but much more professional, and was taken seriously by periodicals like Drama Review magazine, in which I'd read about him back in high school! Anyway, Tahara's daywear consisted of skirts, sandals, and a beard. On stage he would wrap himself in pearls and velvet, and sing opera. At the Cockettes' Academy Award ceremony he won Best Actress for his portrayal of Mother Goose, which is very appropriate because he had a very sweet ladylike quality about him. He hailed from Texas. He grew up playing a little girl clown in a circus where his father worked as a professional rodeo clown.

Jilala (which means "Nuts" in Moroccan) was older than us all, maybe about thirty, and his room looked like the inside of a genie's lamp. He constantly quoted Jean Cocteau, smoked pot, and filmed us with his super-eight camera. He taught me many things about magic and seduction.

Ralph (also known as Raleif or Fifi) and I were always washing huge stacks of dishes and singing old standards at the top of our lungs. He was funny, charming, and loved Brecht and the theater of India. Tahara, Jilala, and Ralph were the true believers in the cult of free theater. They saw it as a service, and to this day they live their lives for other people. I feel lucky to know them.

Jackie, a.k.a. Tacky O. Assis, was a pretty petite biological female with a nasal voice. She had true decadent, tattered, whiny Warhol star appeal. We all sort of had it in for her because she'd gone on a mad rampage and slashed open twenty expensive bags of glitter. One day Beaver walked into her room and found her sitting in front of her vanity mirror painted entirely blue, wearing a Krishna headdress, and fucking herself with a hot dog. Tacky screamed, "Get out! I'm praying!" We may have called her Tacky behind her back but we all liked her. There's something about a real woman doing drag that's very special. There are times when they can do things that queens can't do. Movements. Gestures. Moments. I never realized that until I watched her in slow motion in one of Jilala's films actually becoming Isadora Duncan in a red toga with a big red chiffon scarf.

Harlow was a biological girl groupie who'd been in the Cockettes and had the high distinction of having done Jimmy Page and Jimi Hendrix. They say "Angel Came Down from Heaven" was written about her. She was a dead ringer for Jean Harlow: height, weight, and voice. She was the most beautiful girl I had ever seen with her enormous halo of naturally blonde, curly, fluffy angel hair. She was the only girl Hibiscus had ever slept with, which was quite an achievement. Often she showed up with this little changeling boy who wasn't hers but had a hippie mom somewhere. He was a bit of a terror and would throw fits and scream stuff like, "How come Hibiscus gets to wear eyelashes and I never do?!" Harlow wore green velvet evening gowns with fox furs, green velvet flowers in her hair, and green rhinestone jewelry. Her boudoir was entirely green with green frosted glass crystal leaves hanging around her vanity table. She owned an emerald aqua transparent sequined gown that had belonged to Marlene Dietrich, which she used to let me borrow.

Ruby called himself Greta Garbage. He was a cute young hippie boy who liked intentionally tacky drag. He was routinely bashed on his nightly walk home from The Stud. I remember him saying once, "Tonight I just lay there and let them kick me." He eventually became a callboy in Provincetown.

Jenny was a tiny brunette hippie waif. She'd always be taking off her clothes and dancing, which sometimes got on our nerves, but on the other hand she looked great in a butterfly costume.

Mary and Arthur were the adopted children of the man who invented the Kellogg snack pack. I called them the Kellogg twins. They were beautiful sexy kids with trust funds and they shared their wealth. Mary was a real girl who liked to envision herself as a consort to Mad King Ludwig of Bavaria. She advised me to put a chiffon tent around my bed to improve my love life. I did and it worked! She taught us Hindu dancing in the Panhandle park. Mary had transferable goddess energy, and what feminine mystique I may have now probably goes back to her. Arthur was the one we all wanted. He eventually took up with Link, a slinky, exotic, decadent, druggy Cockette who wrote many of their lyrics. Link went abroad to Europe and then on to the Middle East. He would send us postcards saying, "Where are you? It's magic here." Years later, we heard shocking rumors of a bizarre demise in the Arabian desert. He had allegedly been dragged off by a gang of ruffians, raped, and killed. After that we heard a somewhat less dramatic story about his perishing in Sri Lanka due to inadequate medical care.

Paul Dahling showed up one day with a bottle of Jack Daniels in his hand. He would never say where he came from. Swiftly he went from gawky little boy to sleek hipster. Hot pants! Platforms! Eyelashes! Beaver loved him and would give him great Salvation Army finds, always polka-dots. After acquiring a black monkey fur coat, he began to be courted by the John Waters (the infamous film director who briefly lived in San Francisco) crowd. There were a lot of badass junkies in that group. It was only a matter of time before he got hooked and overdosed on heroin. At the wake there were pictures of him adorning the walls. People were devastated. Over the years I've always thought of Paul whenever some young darling ODs.

Speaking of John Waters, I remember vividly the time we met. It was at Fayette's birthday party. His star, Divine, a three hundred pound female impersonator who appeared in most of his movies, was holding court on the bed and being very friendly. The Angels had just done a show at the Russian River that hadn't gone over well at all. The crowd was too redneck. Waters gave us copious advice, which boiled down to one maxim: "You gotta scare 'em."

Martin was the Grand Kahuna of set design. He was a cute, slender guy with long black hair from an upper class Chinatown family. He had aristocratic Chinese features and an aristocratic Chinese mind. He understood instinctively the Angels' aesthetic — a combination of myth and psychedelia — and designed beautifully detailed, heavily glittered, and totally original sets for us. We spent many an afternoon together at the public library or the Asian Museum researching treasures and making sketches. He called me "Onagata" (kabuki transvestite actress) and was amazed at my ability to pick up straight guys. Once he made a slightly larger than life-sized, papier-mâché baby Buddha's head for me. It was gold. I wore it to the Krishna Festival and danced the Balinese Legong bee dance all afternoon. By '74, he'd progressed to painting huge classically rendered works, the most impressive being a triptych of Bugs Bunny, Porky Pig, and Daffy Duck as the Hindu gods Krishna, Vishnu, and Shiva sitting on lotuses with their eyes absolutely flying out of their heads. Today it supposedly hangs in the Whitney Museum.

Sister Ed had a stern clean face like a Midwestern farm wife or a nun, and in fact he was just out of a monastery. He would wear his monk's robes around the house and always be flashing his jockey shorts at us, eliciting the comment from Hibiscus, "Boy, when they leave the monastery they sure go berserk." He was the original drag queen nun: he'd wear a real habit with 1940s ankle-strap pumps. He was a great housecleaner and very meticulous. He'd spend hours ironing pleats into bolts of chiffon. He was going to inherit a million dollars, or so we thought, and we were all going to move into a windmill in Holland together. He ended up with considerably less but was very generous, not only feeding our glitter habit but renting a limo and taking us to see Marlene Dietrich's final American performance at the Circle Star Theater.

That night at the Circle Star, Wally and John, two genderfuck queens, brought a ton of dumpster flowers that they kept throwing on stage throughout Dietrich's performance. After the show we were allowed backstage because I knew the wardrobe mistress, Annie, from my childhood productions there. Dietrich came out to kiss Beaver's baby and meet us. She saw me in my vintage floor-length, transparent black net, three-tiered evening gown trimmed with a scallop pattern in dark blue sequins, and blue platforms. My hair was pulled into a tight chignon, and Mary had given me her Spanish tortoise-shell comb. My makeup was minimal and I wore a fox fur coat in spite of the raised eyebrows of my animal-loving comrades. That night I realized I was not just a spectacular drag queen but that I could be beautiful as a woman. Dietrich said, "Isn't he gorgeous? He looks like me, only taller." She kissed me on the cheek and I floated on a pink cloud for weeks.

Brian had been a wild kid from a rich family who'd been in a Zen monastery and was very interested in the spiritual side of the Angels. He was straight as an arrow and kind of shy with a sexy butch lisp. There were always a few straight guys around who liked all the attention they could get from the love-starved queens. They often gravitated towards me when it came to sharing the tight sleeping quarters or doing scenes on stage, since the real girls were somewhat aloof, and the other queens were a little bit too anxious. Another one of the straight Angels was Viking Dan.

VIKING DAN

Viking Dan was occasionally arrested
for soliciting on Market Street
He sometimes slept
in my room on Church Street
his classic Teutonic lithe young body
Long blonde hair and light beard

Dorian Gray blue eyes
Detached daydreaming light blue eyes
He shot me with a cardboard bow and arrow
in our pantomime of Cupid and Psyche
in *Myth Thing* the Greek show
We sang "Awake in a Dream"
(I always liked that title)
from the Dietrich film Desire
We were absolute beginners
I hadn't even read Genet or Cocteau
What a perfect first love
He fought a duel over me in *Peking on Acid*
the kabuki show with bongo drums and flutes,
We danced the ice age ballet
Me, the black primeval dragonfly
Me, the Onnagata courtesan fairy Pink Jade
You were the lightning
Teasing and coy you were never far away
Were you drawn to my low burning
feminine screen goddess smolder?
You shared my room on Broderick Street
We met Dietrich together
Around my bed hung a tent
of lavender chiffon
I hung my walls with 1920s beaded gowns
and pictures of us as silent film stars
You made carrot juice in the morning
and fought a duel over me
in the Cowboy show too
You made me look so good ...
I saw you in a soup kitchen in '82
You were living on SSI in the Tenderloin

hanging around pool halls with older gentlemen
You never became a male model
Like me you were just
Poor white trash from Redwood City
You in your Tadzio sailor shirt
and me in my overalls
Yma the mynah bird screaming
"Girl! Girl!" in the kitchen
Erik Satie piano music, Balinese Legong music,
Amid the splendor of the Martin Wong sets
the cardboard glittered swans, planets, palm trees,
Chinese waterfalls, angel wings,
skulls, bunnies and duckies
You were the first in a long stream
of indolent, young, unattainable men
to enter my life, in the sensuous '70s
I read those '70s *Vogues* with pictures of Liza in Paris
Marisa Berenson, and Candy Darling,
I miss everything about the early '70s
Why were they so perfect?
The tinny voice of Josephine Baker
drifting down the hallway
on long hot summer afternoons
If River Phoenix were still alive
he could play you in the movie
perfectly

My first show with the Angels was the Christmas pageant, *Whatever Happened to Baby Jesus?* in 1970. We wanted to use the Poet's Theater (now called the Cable Car) on Mason Street downtown in the Theater District. It was run by Beat poet and publisher Lawrence Ferlinghetti, so we invited him to dinner to obtain his permission.

I was so young and pretty that my fellow Angels decided to use me as bait. They washed and combed and curled my hair, and painted my eyes and lips. They dressed me up in a '30s rayon print dress with vintage ankle-strap platforms, and seated me right next to him like I was supposed to be his date, which is a hoot because he's way straight. Ferlinghetti allowed us to use the theater.

The show was a combination of the Biblical nativity story and The Little Match Girl. I sang Ariel's song from *The Tempest* and got my picture in an alternative paper called the *Good Times*. We quickly followed up with a show called *Myth Thing* based on the Greek myths, with Rodney as Apollo, Beaver as Pandora, Hibiscus as Venus (and Isadora Duncan), his boyfriend Jack as Dionysus, Viking Dan as Cupid/Adonis, Ruby as Narcissus, and me as Psyche. I chose to do Psyche after talking to my sister in Santa Cruz about a new book, *The Female Myth*, an influential tract in early feminism. The show was a simple childlike pageant with joyous singing and dancing, and dazzling glitter sets. It was free, proud, blatant, and homoerotic. We did the show for free, of course, unlike the Cockettes, who we always said were evil for doing "paid" shows.

Holly Woodlawn & Bambi

Platforms and Monkey Furs

I, however, sort of wanted to be in The Cockettes. I wanted to
wear monkey fur and platform shoes and sing old songs. There were
rules against that in the Angels. All your clothes had to be handmade,
and all the songs had to be original. We were Artists! The Cockettes,
on the other hand, were stars! They created havoc! People went
nuts! Word about them spread and they were notorious, even getting
written up in French magazines like *Paris Match* and *Zoom*. They
had more money than we Angels, lots of clothes, lavishly furnished
homes — stuff like an authentic '30s jukebox with bubbles in it! The
Cockettes wanted me to join them too, except for Bobbi Venus (the
same one who threw Hibiscus down a flight of stairs) who put her
foot down and said no. Everyone was understandably afraid to cross
her.

The Cockettes' shows ruled because they were at the Palace Theater, an incredible Deco Chinese movie palace in North Beach with a huge lobby, giant staircases, and Deco chandeliers. The enormous ladies' rooms had couches and full-length mirrors. Inside the theater were long aisles leading to the enormous proscenium hung with long amber-lit satin curtains. Thousands of people in high drag lined the street waiting to get in. Vintage cars pulled up at midnight to klieg lights and out came the Cockettes, featuring the Cockette look: shaved eyebrows, glitter eye makeup, long satin bias-cut gowns (the bias cut makes the fabric clingy and sexy, and looks really '30s), vintage platform heels, Deco jewelry. Hair was slicked back, then exploded into a giant Afro in back. Think Karen Black in the movie *Day of the Locust*. The shows were pastiches of old movies, with glittered Deco sets made of cardboard. Peter's transcendental piano playing lent an air of sophisticated style and class to the proceedings.

The Cockettes were glamorous, yet still really gross. The opulence and grotesquery existed side by side. People may have dressed up like fashion models from the 1930s but they'd be drinking Jack Daniels, eating quaaludes, and falling off their platforms onto their heads. There were conflicts within the Cockettes about the proper ratio of beauty to crassness. One Cockette used to say, "Most of the fans would rather see us get up in high drag and take a shit on stage." They'd do routines like *Spanky & Our Gang*, only they called it *Smacky & Our Gang*. In the skit, the kids wrote the schoolteacher's phone number on the chalkboard, and next to it they wrote, "Mrs. Rodel sucks good dick." The teacher walked into the classroom and shrieked, "OH!" then "...That number's been changed," and she wrote down her new number. Another show called *Pearls Over Shanghai* was set in China in 1940. It featured the sexiest, most aggressive, and salacious performances I'd ever seen. John Rothermel as the jaded lady and Bobbi Venus as the American singer were sooo intense. The

'40s hairdos and spike platforms made everyone look like perverse Vargas girls. The show, in which sex workers demanded freedom, became a rallying cry for legalizing prostitution.

The Cockettes weren't just a performance troupe, they hung out together. They'd do things like hold afternoon parties where everyone dressed up like '40s club ladies with little white gloves, and shared hors d'ouevres and cocktails. They had parties after every show, and we Angels would always be there. The rest of the time we all hung out at the Shed, or the Stud, or Hamburger Mary's. Though we were friends there was a rivalry exacerbated by their blatant thievery of our show ideas. Right after we did *Myth Thing*, they did *Hot Greeks*. Hello? The Cockettes used to plan orgies that I never went to but heard about. There was a little bit of savagery to their sex lives. Real primitivism. For example, the time Tommy, Peter's boyfriend, had his dick bitten into by Miguel, or the time Link rammed his five-inch nails up Angel Jack's ass.

Sylvester and a few of the Cockettes lived at The Chateau, an apartment above the Upper Market Street Gallery where they often had parties. Sylvester and I instantly bonded when I outdressed him at the famous Club Mandarin party by wearing a sky blue satin 1936 evening gown, unbelievable maroon velvet ankle straps with silver piping, and a black wool-belted coat trimmed in black Persian lamb. My hair was gelled and skinned back into a tight bun with a huge brown Afro hairpiece attached. He said I looked like Charlotte Rampling in *The Damned*. Club Mandarin was incredible, the quintessential Cockette party. It cost fifteen dollars to get in, which was a fortune in those days. Everyone was dressed to the nines in vintage clothes. There was a sultry, smoky-voiced, cigarette girl right out of the old movies named Heather Nipplepinch. Peter played on a baby grand all night long. Sylvester and Rothermel did long sets as did Inez, in a French accent no less, after which she left in a 1927 Lincoln. After these incredible performances, different people were asked to sing and I, the mystery woman, got my turn. Then there was dancing and more drinking. At the height of the evening, everyone sang along to "The Varsity Drag" and formed a kick line. For the next half hour there was a spontaneous sing-along.

The party continued the next night. I lent Sylvester my coat and he lent me his crepe satin gold bias-cut gown. We were the same size! John Rothermel dressed up in Chinese opera drag, but by the end of the evening he had managed to lose all his clothes. As people were departing, he was making love to a pretty long-haired boy on the dance floor. I thought it was quite lovely.

After that night, Sylvester and I traded clothes and boyfriends all the time. I loved his room, hung with velvet and pictures of Garbo and the De Marcos, a steamy 1930s husband and wife tango team. On stage, Sylvester was so gorgeous, so feminine, so tall. He sang like Lena Horne and looked like a Nubian goddess. He always made us feel like we were at the Cotton Club, singing "Sleepy Time Down South" and "Harlem On My Mind." Sylvester was three years older than me, and a real role model. I was determined to become like him.

NUBIAN GODDESS

I saw Sylvester one night at a party
(he was thin then) descending a staircase
He was wearing long Garbo slacks, a tropical vintage shirt,
fox coat, and a turban
He looked radiant and said, "I just had sex with Leon Russell."

I saw Sylvester getting off a bus at Market and Castro
He had an Afro, cutoff shorts, and platform shoes
He said, "Me and my girls the Pointer Sisters are going to London with Rod Stewart."

I saw Sylvester at the Upper Market Street Gallery one afternoon
He had just gotten back from L.A. and was being escorted
everywhere in limousines
He showed me a vintage '20s gown he'd just bought
He said, "I just met Deborah Walley from
... Bleach Blanket Something."
(It was the Deborah Walley, from *Gidget Goes Hawaiian.*)

I saw Sylvester in front of the Palace Theater one night
He was wearing a tropical print '30s rayon dress, a fox fur coat,
and six-inch cork wedgies
I asked where he got his dress and he said, "Oh, it was a gift."

I saw Sylvester in a big hat, in flowing robes, on Polk Street,
walking his two Borzoi dogs
He said, "We're looking for someone to buy us cocktails."

I saw Sylvester on Halloween night on Polk Street
in a blue sequin gown
with a huge cotton candy beehive wig, wrapped in blue tulle
And he didn't have to say anything.

Another big influence was John Rothermel. He could croon like
Bing and belt like Merman while maintaining a unique smoldering,
mocking stage presence. He sang a lot of Mae West songs and
definitely had her walk down pat. He often wore big platinum
blonde Afro wigs with antique silver fish-scale sequined gowns, or
tight whore dresses with fishnet stockings, ankle strap platforms,
'40s hair, and black monkey fur coats. Monkey fur coats were very
chic in the '30s, and became the ultimate '70s statement here in
San Francisco, and in New York among the Warhol set. On stage he

was a sight to see in his huge feathered hat with a long transparent gown, revealing his rather large silver glittered dick, dangling like the Krupp diamond.

Fayette was a real girl with long red hair past her hips who had been Little Miss Asbury Park, New Jersey as a child. She was notorious for her hats that featured not only the usual birds and flowers, but on one occasion (a Led Zeppelin concert, as I recall) a lobster. Her boyfriend was Tomata who hailed from Seattle where he'd been in the Whiz Kids, the local version of the Cockettes. Another couple, Scrumbly Koldewyn (who wrote many beautiful Cockettes songs) and Sweet Pam, had pictures of their wedding on Mount Tamalpais appear in *Rolling Stone* magazine.

The Cockettes featured two pre-op transsexuals, Bobbi Venus and Dahlia, who were excruciatingly beautiful and inspired many young sissies to go on hormones, though not me at that point, as I was scared of what it might do to my sex drive. Bobbi looked like a 1930s *Vogue* magazine evening gown model, a young knockout beauty. She was the first pre-op transsexual I ever met and the most beautiful. She strutted around with her nose in the air, a vixen spoiled by adoring fans. She was also a hairdresser and did all the wigs. She hated me. I had made one too many spectacular entrances for her, plus I could sing and tap dance. I was dangerous. Years later Bobbi moved to L.A. to work at the Queen Mary Lounge, then toured with Judy Carne as a member of her backup chorus and personal assistant, her gender status raising a few eyebrows here and there. It's the glass ceiling for transsexuals, no matter how beautiful you is, always somebody gonna know. I heard she finally moved to Las Vegas, married a cop, and worked her way up to become the leading showgirl at the Tropicana's Moulin Rouge. Rumor has it that she carried on a brief affair with Sylvester Stallone, and that she eventually left Vegas and worked as a background actress in *Star Trek: The Next Generation*.

Dahlia was as sweet as Bobbi was mean. She was very funny and got a scholarship to study acting at the American Conservatory Theater. She looked like none other than the young Liz Taylor in her magenta satin platforms, jet black hair slicked back then exploding into a mass of curls, a white bias-cut gown, Certainly Red lips, and a real baby doll voice. She ended up getting a sex change (as did Bobbi) and moving to San Diego to become a stripper in sailor bars. She got married in the '80s but her husband died in a bike accident, and now she lives in Hawaii with her mother. Looking back, I envision Dahlia in *Tinsel Tarts*, holding a suitcase, standing at a glittered bus stop. She has become to me Lady Stardust, L-O-L-A, the symbol of the glitter generation. My generation.

The Cockettes went to New York City in 1972 to play the Andersen Theater on the Lower East Side. Rex Reed set it up. The show didn't do so well, apparently because they partied a bit too much at Jacqueline Susann's apartment before opening night. Legend has it that Angela Lansbury got up and walked out during the first ten minutes of the show followed by her whole queeny entourage. Gore Vidal supposedly wrote in the *New York Times*, "Just having no talent is not enough." I've heard the Cockettes were told point blank by their producers that if they fired half the cast and went professional they'd get a run Off Broadway. They declined to break up their family, which is to their credit, but I've always felt they should have stayed and made their mark because they were the most talented queens that ever were. After that fiasco, they plucked everyone by coming home to perform the best show they ever did, the Paris show, *Jewels of Midnight*. The set was a giant mylar vanity mirror. They descended a big ol staircase in the opening number one by one, each in a different color Deco perfume bottle-top headdress with matching feathered boas.

Meanwhile, back at the Angels of Light commune, things were going great for us little Angels until suddenly some kids from

Mission High burned our house down to the ground. They had been harassing us for weeks, hanging around, once even pulling a knife on someone. We called the cops but they refused to help us. Even the real girls had no influence with them. One day we smelled something funny. The kids had broken the gas main. We grabbed what we could carry and ran for our lives. The house caught fire and a lot of stuff was lost forever, including a priceless collection of Maxfield Parrish prints I had on loan from my old pal Byron.

After the fire Hibiscus decided to move to New York. He'd had been stung by a recent spate of bad reviews taking him to task for stage hogging and general egomania. Losing his home was the last straw. He also wanted to marry his boyfriend Jack, a cute teddy bear of a guy, who was from a wealthy family in Short Hills, New Jersey. The two of them had a tempestuous relationship full of fighting, histrionics, and violence. Very old school, very Lana Turner. They were married on stage in New York in a huge extravaganza, *Enchanted Miracle*. Not only was Allen Ginsberg in the show, but Hibiscus's family was, too. The show debuted their glitter twin drag act (for the next three years they were always dressed alike) and ended as they drove off in an opulent Cinderella-style coach.

After the fire, I moved in with some of the other more zen-like Angels to what soon became our new headquarters in the Haight, the top floor of a beautiful Victorian house on the corner of Broderick and Page. There we became more involved in the network of communes that still persisted in the Haight-Ashbury, and increasingly across northern California. The Summer of Love was very much over; this was after the Manson murders. There were speed freaks everywhere. Girls couldn't walk alone at night in the Haight. It was 1972, but the counterculture was still going strong.

Unfortunately, it was still hard to get a job with long hair or if you were out of the closet. Not that we wanted to. There weren't nonprofits and health food stores and other cool places to work with dignity back then. The result was that people banded together with their food stamps and welfare checks to live cheaply. I literally lived well on eighty dollars a month, with a little help from my friends. Needless to say, this would just not be possible for anyone today.

Anyway, there were all these predominantly gay communes: Hunga Dunga, Kali-Flower, Wolf Creek, and maybe about eight others. We were all linked together by our common circumstances and bizarre food necessities. We needed mega-healthy type stuff; we couldn't just shop at Safeway. Every month a fellow named Lizard from Hunga Dunga would gather together all the welfare checks and drive out with some other handsome hippie boys to the farmers' market and buy lots of brown rice, tofu, and produce to deliver to the various communes. One rule we had about food was that you could never serve yourself (unless there was nobody else home), you had to find someone to serve you. I think it was an idea they'd gotten from Jean Cocteau, and it was related to the philosophy of living for others. I found it charming at the time, and still do. There were all sorts of rules at the communes, the most extreme of which was at Kali-Flower where if you wanted to have sex with someone, he or she had to be approved by the entire commune. They had one giant room where everyone slept and/or had sex. No privacy. No walls. Tearing down walls was very important at the communes, creating communal space. Equally important was not tearing down the beams, so the roof didn't cave in.

Irving was the Karl Marx of the commune network; it was his vision. He looked like a Gurdjieff character with a beard, long hair, and long flowing robes. He had wise looking, heavy lidded eyes, and a soft but authoritative voice. Irving was friends with pre-Warhol gay cult film director Jack Smith, and appeared in his famous film, *Flaming Creatures*. Irving had written a book called *Sheeper*, a lot of which was about taking acid with another pal, Allen Ginsberg. He set up Kali-Flower in a huge house in the Western Addition with high ceilings, a beautiful garden, and industrial-size ovens in the basement for baking bread that they distributed for free to the poor. This was part of Irving's philosophy, a mixture of Hinduism and Celtic magic. Everything had to be for free. It was the cult of free. They decorated the place with kitschy old bible study posters, and the boys often wore brown Franciscan friar robes. It was an amazing mixture of high camp and authentic spirituality.

Irving was a photographer, and I was once summoned to his house and spent six hours trying to achieve the wistful timeless look of Dietrich for him. He would say, "Johnny, think of eons and eons of lost love, but with a will to go on." He gave me a real lesson in diva-matics: you can never be too soft.

Kali-Flower also printed up beautiful homemade monthly newspapers that they'd deliver bound in yarn. They were printed on a press that Irving had gotten from a wealthy New York woman who'd been introduced to him by a legendary heroin addict in Manhattan. Their paper not only reviewed Angels and Cockettes shows, they had a whole section on Asshole Consciousness. Toilet paper was definitely frowned upon; one had to wash one's anus thoroughly with water. This was, I think, related to the high regard in which they placed the sex act known as rimming. Visitors to the communes were often put off by this. If the lack of toilet paper wasn't enough to scare off outsiders, some of the other practices were. After a child was born in a commune, it was traditional for all the members to gather together and ritualistically eat the placenta after it had been stir-fried in a wok with brown rice and vegetables. A lactating mother was also wont to be asked for a jar of her milk. It was a commune; we shared everything!

The Angels commune was a spin-off from Kali-Flower for people who couldn't quite live up to Irving's standards of selflessness. Our commune was more fun oriented, more self-indulgent. My stardust memories of this era are truly ethereal. The silver-painted kitchen and refrigerator. Sitting on the roof on acid watching the stars till 3 a.m. Fred Astaire movies on television. The sound of sewing machines making shimmering fabrics into endless show-stopping costumes.

Dear reader, please don't think that because of all the lefty, commie, veggie, spiritual, counterculture stuff that we didn't have our Apollonian/Dionysian scales perfectly balanced. Our high ideals were tempered with extreme hedonism. I really miss the bath houses. The Ritch Street Baths was in its heyday. Buddy Night was a good night because you could walk up to some guy and say, "Wanna be my buddy?" and get in for two bucks. My friend Damian from the Rainbow Gypsies and I would often sneak in through the fire escape, walk in naked (leaving our clothes on the roof), and steal towels from the bathroom. There were private rooms, an orgy room, and a TV room where people would watch Johnny Carson (back then there were no VCRs for porn films). You could get a nice avocado and sprouts sandwich at the snack bar, or relax in the hot tub. I was especially talented at cruising. I'd case the joint for the best-looking guys. When I saw one I liked I'd race around so that I could nonchalantly pass him going the opposite direction and strike up a conversation. I was one of the brazen forerunners at transgendering in the baths. You weren't allowed in wearing drag, of course, though Sylvester could get away with smuggling beaded gowns in and changing in his room. He was also famous for putting bubble bath in the showers, creating a massive wall of bubbles from which he could then grab "numbers." Normally I brushed my Louise Brooks bob back, boy style. One night though, I was heavily cruised by what looked to be a studly Italian straight guy. He told me about meeting a beautiful transvestite at the Midnight Sun (he liked queens) and going home with her. The tranny's Mafioso boyfriend came home while he was there and he had to hide in the closet till the coast was clear. As he told me this story, I slowly pulled my hair down, crossed my legs, and tried to look feminine. We went back to his room and made mad, beautiful, passionate love. It was one of my first real lady-boy sex experiences.

Onnagata Inamorata

Without Hibiscus, the focus of the Angels became more cerebral and poetic, less pagan. We began work on a kabuki show called *Peking On Acid*. It started with Beaver as a kabuki frog, hopping through a vision of skulls, bunnies, and duckies. I was a black dragonfly. Rodney was a lion with huge butterfly wings. Two cavemen emerged through the gates of the Forbidden City, representing the seven chakras of the Hindu Kundalini. We each picked a chakra and a color scheme to work with. I was the heart chakra. I wore twelve-inch wooden platform clog shoes portraying a fantastic giant insect goddess bringing an end to war.

I was also the sex chakra since everyone else was a little bit too shy. They all said, "Let Miss Johnny do it." I seized the opportunity. I appeared as a kabuki onnagata courtesan in a pleasure garden, making love to her swain (played by the deliciously beautiful Robert Altman, not the director, the porn star). I did my set with airbrushed Chinese orchids, which had sperm-shaped squiggles coming out of them. My costume was a handmade kimono in grey and violet with three layers of stuffed kapok rolls for piping around the hems, covered in stuffed orchid appliqués, and topped with a huge white wig down to my elbows. Robert was draped in bolts of royal blue silk velvet, with kabuki makeup, and his hair in a topknot. We reenacted a series of erotic tableaus in stylized puppet-like kabuki movements. In a moment of inspiration I pulled a bamboo flute out of his pants as if it were a phallus and began playing it. What a clever girl I was! This show, luckily caught on 8mm film, took three months to create, and was grandly realized in an outdoor park setting in Diamond Heights.

While doing research for the show, I discovered a huge book of Asian erotic art. I would suggest that any queen who has an interest in sex look this stuff up. The Hindu and Buddhist cultures have a long, long history of open healthy sexuality, including a good dose of transsexuality. I learned about the tradition of the cut sleeve (a Chinese emperor when getting up cut the sleeve of his silk robe so that he wouldn't awaken his young boy lover), and erotic Chinese fairy tales including The Secret Fairy and the fairy fires.

While you're at the library, why not check out a few classics like Jean Genet's *Our Lady of the Flowers*, *Last Exit To Brooklyn* by Hubert Selby, Jr., and John Rechy's *City of Night*? The three transvestite characters from these novels — Divine, Georgette, and Miss Destiny — are important archetypes.

In Genet's book, Divine is a saint-like romantic streetwalker who lives in a Parisian garret and meets her boyfriend in jail. When I first read the book, I was surprised to learn that there were people like me in the '40s. I found her world very seductive.

Selby portrays Georgette as a young hip queer who lives at home with her mother in Brooklyn. She has an abusive thug boyfriend.

In Rechy's novel, Miss Destiny is a brassy, redheaded, punkish prostitute on L.A.'s Sunset Strip. They're not pretty stories, and they map out a lowlife world that I've always tried to keep away from. Fortunately I came out in the '70s and have never had to deal with the sort of heavy repression that make these tales so grim. Having been written in the '40s, '50s, and '60s, these characters have a lot of negative characteristics, but they are essential to the understanding of the development of the transvestite mystique. Bambi Lake, my persona, is a creation with a specific agenda: to provide a positive archetype.

We did a few more beautiful Angels shows at the University of California Extension building in the lower Haight, including *The Cowboy Show* that contained the best scene ever. The covered wagons were crossing the plains, and we were using shopping carts as covered wagons. A rumbling was heard offstage and suddenly someone screamed, "Buffalo stampede!" For ten minutes people ran across the stage with cardboard buffalos. It may have been the funniest scene I've ever been in.

One day when I was sitting in my room playing Joni Mitchell songs on my guitar, a friend of the commune's, mad speed freak poet Michael, slithered into my room. He said, "Hey, Johnny, I've written you a song." He proceeded to sing me a deranged Mick Jagger-esque blues song that I could never imagine myself singing. Now it seems to have a flawless appeal.

Well, my number is six hundred
Sixty and six
And if you got my number
then you can have your kicks

Ooh I'm goin' down
Well, I don't mind dyin'

But I hate to leave you
Hangin' round

Well, I'm not just a Swiss girl
But I'll tell you what I'll do
I'll fix your clockwork for you
And I'll blow your Alp horn too

Ooh, I'm goin' down
Well, I don't mind dyin'
But I hate to leave you
Hangin' round

I don't care if your paw was mean
And I don't care if your teeth are green
And I don't care if you're just sixteen
Just keep the temple clean
Baby, just keep the temple clean

There were many things about gay life I had yet to learn. One day Fayette told me in a rather matter-of-fact way that Viking Dan was in jail for prostitution. I was devastated. "Why would he turn tricks downtown?" I asked, all innocence.

"Money," she replied. "And maybe he likes it." I'd gotten used to being around all the drinking, drugs, dealing, nudie parties, promiscuity, and faux whorishness. But beautiful Viking behind bars? This didn't compute. Well, I was about to learn just how easy it is to wind up in the slammer.

One day I was walking home from the Kali-Flower commune, through the lively and colorful Western Addition ghetto when a police paddy wagon pulled up beside me. My mind was still on the Gertrude Stein opera, *In Circles*, which I had just heard for the first time in the garden with Irving. I was featuring a severe 1920s Louise Brooks bob/China Doll haircut, Chinese pajamas, and groovy New York suede platform Keds. Was this the 1990s? No, it was 1972, thank you very much. The cops began verbally harassing me, yelling, "Hey you, bitch, come here. What's your street name? Are you working? Don't you know it's against the law to dress like that?"

Not knowing any better I sassed them, screaming in indignation, "I haven't done anything wrong! Leave me the hell alone! I don't have a street name, I'm not a Tenderloin hooker, I live in the Haight and I'm going home!" They said I had an attitude problem, threw me in the back of the wagon where there were two more cops beating an old drunk black man with billy clubs while demanding to know where he got his drugs. After the cops left the back of the wagon, he threw up a bag of speed. It was not pretty. They eventually put me in a holding tank for a couple of hours with a lot of crazy people. The cells were right in the office, like some sheriff's office on *Gunsmoke*. I learned that realness in drag could be dangerous. I was not in glitter or feathers; I was not putting on a show. I got in trouble because I was "serving tranny." To top it off, a few months later beautiful Dahlia of the Cockettes was arrested for soliciting at Enrico's in North Beach, where she'd been working as a topless dancer. I started to wonder what on earth was going on.

Bambi with Cafe Megalomania

Up, Up, and Away

Meanwhile, Hibiscus formed the New York Angels of Light. He met Maurice, legendary choreographer of the Belgian ballet, who was able to get *Enchanted Miracle* booked in London. It was 1972. Hibiscus called Beaver, Rodney, Sister Ed, and me to join him there. I played Cleopatra and Isadora Duncan. At the end of my Isadora scene I threw my top off to reveal my breasts, which were simply painted on. We slept right in the theater for the show's two-week run, and got wonderful reviews. I loved London, and remained in town after the show closed.

I initially stayed with two Angels, Gregory and Tchandra, who were living there. After a few months though, I moved to youth hostels, and even tried the squat system. Squatting was unpleasant, the people were obsessed with dogmatic anarchist politics and very cold. There was also no way as an American that I could ever get by using as little hot water as they expected me to. During this time I worked as a dishwasher and waiter, often in rather slave-like conditions. British people would rudely imitate my nasal California accent. But those were the drawbacks.

On the positive side, there was sex with skinheads by moonlight in Hampstead Heath. Every night. Seeing Nico in concert. Hanging out on Kings Road with glitter and crazy color hair everywhere. The underground subway was covered in posters for the original stage production of *The Rocky Horror Picture Show* in Chelsea, which I saw and loved. I took a course in tambour weaving, a crochet method of hand beading, at the Oxford Circus Institute of Fashion. I sat in a giant room full of black ladies with thick Scottish brogues. I created a black sequin gown with silver stars.

Despite the ascendancy of glam rock, I still noticed that the few drag queens who dared go out in public got hassled, so I spent my entire stay as a boy; with the exception of a job I got at the Grand Magic Circus of Paris. I was originally working as an usher, and began making money on the side teaching the cast claquette, tap dance. Twice then, when the beautiful black girl who played Josephine Baker took ill, I was her replacement. I wore a brown body stocking, chocolate brown base makeup, rhinestone eye makeup, an enormous white ostrich feather opera coat with a six-foot train (talk about drag)… and bananas.

After a year, Hibiscus called from America to say his new show, *Razzamatazz*, was opening in Provincetown. So I came back. It was 1973. You know, glitter, New York Dolls, All The Young Dudes, Alladin Sane, the Pointer Sisters: "Yes we can, yes we can, yes we can, can."

Every singer has to find a song that brings good luck. The first song that ever did that for me was "Kiss Me" from the noirish Marilyn Monroe movie *Niagra*. I did it in *Razzamatazz*, stepping out onto the stage in my blonde wig and new hand-beaded gown to solo piano accompaniment. It was the only serious number in the midst of a wild loud colorful drag show, and it brought the house down every time. A pattern was starting. I was the melancholy note in a sea of giddiness. The show was exceptional. It starred not only Hibiscus and Jack but his three little sisters, ages sixteen, eleven, and nine, and his mother as Glinda the Good Witch in a costume that lit up with twinkling electric lights. The audiences were charmed to see a gay child and his family working together in a vaudevillian style. There was tap dancing and burlesque: it was very George M. Cohan influenced. Very *Gypsy*. It was a sharp contrast to the decadence of the Cockettes or the Waters and Warhol crowds.

P-town, Funtown USA, was awash with old school drag stars performing in chic little nightspots: legendary Lynn Carter, who did her fierce Phyllis Diller impersonation along with fast, campy, bitchy monologues; the great Arthur Blake, doing his *Arthur Blake Follies* at the Back Door, with a chorus line of muscle boys in bikinis and feather headdresses. Bette Davis herself had always preferred Blake's impersonation of her over Charles Pierce's. Arthur Blake also performed with Jayne Mansfield in her notorious Las Vegas act.

But the Queen of the older queens that summer was Wayland Flowers with his fabulous puppet, Madame. He performed at the Angels' welcoming party at the Owl's Nest hotel. After our show on opening night, he made a point of coming up to me. After making strong eye contact, he draped his arm around my shoulder, and said, "Never give up! You have it!" I have always remembered that during difficult times.

PROVINCETOWN (ALMOST FIRE ISLAND)

Ritzy titzy New England
Lesbian Bed & Breakfasts

Free Quiche
Black Manhattan Marsha
who'd been at Stonewall
interviewed on national TV
the bottles flying behind her
She arrived on the bus
in full fairytale drag, she said
"I wanted to freak 'em out on the buuus"
rubbing elbows with
the Warhol and the Waters crowds
Dancing on tables
at the Back Door
and the Boat Slip
The show and me a hit
Commercial Street
packed with people
the Three Degrees and the Sexolettes
Monty Rock the Third
Get Dancin'
bounding out of discos
Rock the Boat
I slept with sexy East Coast punks
Cookie Mueller won a Halloween Contest
dressed as Sharon Tate with
a bloody baby doll
pinned to her stomach
sand and sea, clam chowder
Holly Woodlawn was so sweet
she changed my life

Razzamatazz was a hit and was booked for a tour of Europe. On
the way we did a few weeks' run at the New York Theater Ensemble

in Manhattan. Off Off Broadway. After the show, I stayed in a gallery on St. Mark's Place owned by the pianist from the Angels, and worked washing dishes in little Italy. I really loved Manhattan: Bloomingdale's, the Odessa, and the Continental Baths. Oh, the Continental Baths! The Provincetown hustlers would live in the cubicles for weeks at a time. The best-looking hustlers I've ever seen in my life. The place was enormous. The men were enormous. The pool was enormous. Men from Yale and Harvard. And drag shows! Beautiful, wonderful, mahhhvelous.

My friend, Tomata du Plenty, was living in New York at the time. He had a cable access TV show where he and his girlfriend Fayette would dress up like Nancy and Sluggo from the old comic strip. He was also masterminding something called the *New Live Berlin Sex Act*, which they performed in between up-and-coming bands like Blondie, Talking Heads, and the Ramones at CBGB, New York's premier punk club. They were very campy. One show was called *Savage VooDoo Nuns*, and once they had a drag queen (actually, the most insane Cockette of them all, John Flowers) wrestling with someone in an alligator suit.

It was Tomata who introduced me and the New York Angel Miss Charles when we put on a show together at the gallery. Miss Charles and I were becoming a fierce team. We'd worked together in *Razzmatazz* and we were both mean little scene stealers. For our show I called myself Nazimova Bossanova and Miss Charles became Julie English. I opened up with "Blame It on the Bossanova," naturally. We also sang songs by Brecht, did the theme from *A Man and a Woman*, the theme from *La Strada* by Nino Rota, and various Julie London numbers. That was the first night, the '60s night.

The second night was devoted to Joni Mitchell. I sang five of her songs accompanied by a guitarist. We wore dresses we got from Sayeed, a neighbor in the fashion business. I knew Sayeed because he'd hired me to do fashion designs for him. I drew everything

Marilyn Monroe and Rita Hayworth had ever worn in the movies; at two dollars a sketch I earned about eight hundred bucks. He gave me a Giorgio di Sant'Angelo white crepe sheath gown with translucent sleeves with rhinestones on them that Nancy Kissinger had worn just the other night. Miss Charles wore a black Oscar de la Renta peasant evening gown with a full circle gypsy skirt that Jackie Kennedy had worn earlier that week.

Finally, it was off to Amsterdam with us and the show.

THE GRAND TOUR

I flew off to Europe
a beautiful young queen
off to see the world
there's such a lot of world to see
I just had to stay
in London
To experience the grey skies
the year of the Diamond Dogs
Bowie on sax
Twiggy at Biba
Brown lipstick and
Satin, Deco
Glitter Rock was an
English thing
I just had to shop for
platforms
buy vintage tea gowns and
hats at Maria's
on King's Road
where Bianca shopped
At the movies

I saw Holly in
Andy Warhol's *Trash*
and started to consider going on
hormones
Next stop Holland, Showtime
Windmills, sexy Nordic men
Hashish, nightlife
choo choo trains,
the Milkveg, D.O.K.
Shopping,
Studio Fong Ling,
Myerheels
the ultimate shoe store
catering to red light
district hookers
hundreds of styles and colors
of Barbie doll pumps
we modeled in magazines
we sang in cabarets
we had sex in Vandell Park
coffee at the Hotel American
ladies in schneckens
and pleated evening smocks
On to France
the Nancy Theater Festival
in the quaintest French pensione
straight out of Collette
Sugar and I
in that little doll house room
with a bidet, green shutters
We met Mitterand
Hibiscus's little sisters

in lace garter belts in candy colors
peach, mint, lavender
from the naughty
French lingerie shops
we feared being kidnapped
we ate quiche

Each night I stopped the show when I did my number. In Berlin, we played at the Akademie der Künste. We were put up in a fancy hotel with gigantic rooms and a balcony with a wrought iron railing overlooking a beautiful strasse. I will never forget the ornate dining room that had a fat German businessman passed out drunk at the breakfast table. Romy Haag, Germany's reigning queen, saw the show at the Academy and offered me twice what I was making to quit and work for her. She also invited Miss Charles. We didn't say yes right away because we were waiting for this old bejewelled dowager to decide whether she wanted to take the *Razzamatazz* troupe to Monte Carlo.

As soon as that fell through we jumped at the opportunity to work at her charming club, Chez Romy Haag. We went off to Berlin and gave Romy our passports so she could get us work permits. This sort of made us captives. We couldn't leave Germany, and had to miss the Paris dates for Razzamatazz. John Rothermel had to be flown in to replace me. Miss Charles and I rechristened ourselves "Sugar Candy" and "Beverly Hills." I was Beverly. And so began my year in Berlin.

Bambi & Freddy

Ice Queens of Berlin

The show at Romy Haag's was called *Viva Les Boys*. It was a very professional, fast moving, high energy show, combining French music hall, German cabaret, proto-MTV type rock numbers, as well as old standard American gay bar tunes from Shirley Bassey and Bette Midler. It was all strictly lip synch and pantomime, "playback," they called it. The clientele was a mixture of fresh German college kids, shop girls, transsexual strippers, pimps, male prostitutes, aristocrats, artists, and tourists. I had many stage door Johnnys, who hung around and waited till I got off at dawn. They were young cute hustler types who liked only queens. I called them "queen fuckers." Romy's wasn't a gay club at all, it was a queen fucker club. It was also like a drag finishing school where you learned both show drag (wig, big makeup, big presentation), and street drag (a more subtle, stylish, modern, workable female look). I loved the hormoned-out bitchy glamour of it all. We weren't secretaries here… we were showgirls!

In a cruel twist of fate, shortly after we arrived in Germany, we got a call from Hibiscus telling us that a Brazilian drag troop called "Zee Croquettes" had arrived in Paris, and were majorly upstaging the Angels of Light debut. As you might guess from the name, they were a thinly veiled rip-off of the Cockettes. Hibiscus and Rothermel caught their show in one of the most prestigious theaters in town, the Bobino Club, where Josephine Baker had played. They opened a week after she passed away. Hibiscus and Rothermel sat mournfully in the balcony watching the audience go nuts for their plagiarized concepts. They went backstage and were startled to discover the *Zoom* magazine photos of the real Cockettes all over the dressing room, and the Croquettes sitting there copying the makeup. "We love zee American Cockettes. San Francisco! We take their name, we take their faces, we make ze dancing!" Their trump card was that they were incredible dancers, and sexy Brazilians to boot. They were spotted by Liza Minelli, who was quoted in the press as saying they were absolutely fabulous. Their show ran for years and they all made a handsome living off it. It was every Cockette's and Angel's dream to make it in Paris and now that would never be. I learned then that you had to strike while the iron is hot, and never take anything for granted in the trendy world of underground theater.

Our new boss, Romy, was rich, powerful, and glamorous. Chez Romy Haag's was the hottest spot in town. She was Dutch, and had gone to Paris at age fifteen to work at the Carrousel and the Alcazar. Romy achieved international fame when Claudia Cardinale tore her wig off, enraged by the dead-on impersonation of her. She even suspected that Romy was signing autographs in her name. After ten years as the vedette (center chorus girl) at the Alcazar and being wined and dined by the likes of Aristotle Onassis, she opened her club in Berlin. She had furs, diamonds, a penthouse apartment:

very Helmut Newton. I was impressed. Dahlia and Bobbi had given me the idea but it was Romy who really convinced me to go on hormone shots and start developing tits. She said, "I don't like you as a boy," and assured me I could still get a hard-on. She also said, "You vill alvays haf sailors." Boy, was that prophetic! The navies of both Germany and America (and probably other nations as well) have a shadowy tradition of camaraderie with transvestites and transsexuals.

I had reached the crossroads of my life. Generally speaking, my life has unfolded into two major sections: pre-hormonal and post-hormonal. Before the hormones, I was a thin and somewhat shy, moonish, melancholy boy. The new me was to become fuller figured, happier, and sexier. For the last four years I had spent sleepless nights deliberating over the decision to go on hormones. Happy ending. But… I was soon to find out that this decision had unforeseen consequences.

I became paranoid about my body. I had to grow in my beard, and go through the elaborate and very painful process of facial waxing with Elizabeth Arden's patented depilatory wax. I became hyper-aware of my narrow hips, height (6'3" in heels), facial hair, nose, thin lips *ad infinitum*. Could I pass or would these "flaws" give me away, or make me a wallflower? There were a lot of men in Berlin I was very interested in.

At Romy's, there was a gang of big *Tom of Finland* studs with names like Apollo and Samson. They came every night, arriving on Harley Davidsons or in Rolls Royces. They were known as the "zuhälter," or pimps. They were straight but enjoyed our wicked feminine illusions: feathers, high heels, sequins, wigs, and perfume. They would tease and taunt us with their hot sexy bodies, but they didn't want you unless you were like Romy (who'd had them all, of course) with big tits, cheekbones, money, furs, etc. You had to be careful not to offend them or get them angry as they were rather dangerous. Boy, were they hot!

They had their own hangout across town called the Borzolino, a place with legalized prostitution. Their girls worked the johns at the bar and there were beds right upstairs. Shirley Bassey music played as the zuhälter prowled about. One night the cutest one invited me into the men's room. I declined gracefully. I was a lady now! I kept to the lower league boys, the "strichers" who worked the circuit dating American tourists or the abundance of male johns in town. The strichers had their own bars, and when Hibiscus entered one in boy drag, he had five drinks bought for him in two minutes. Dating German men was a real education for me, and a great release after all those years of pining after straight men. As a boy I was never really attractive to the sort of men I liked. Now I had breasts from the hormone shots, and I learned about the joys of she-male sex.

I had been aware from San Francisco days that it was pretty easy for a nelly gay man to get laid by hot butch gay guys. The Cockettes eroticized dicks under skirts with stockings, heels, etc. and made out like bandits. I'd gone that route, but now I saw a new frontier. Actual heterosexual men. Having tits put me over the top. I was no longer attractive to gay men, but I was attractive to straight guys who were perhaps a little bit gay or even just curious. The next step would be to go for a complete sex change operation and become interesting only to completely straight men. If I'd had the money I would have done it in a minute: straight men will let me girl-out during sex. Gay men get turned off by that. With a straight man I can be as fishy as I want, and scream, "Daddy! Daddy! Daddy!" at the height of passion, or roll my hips and shoulders like Rita Hayworth.

My first straight men were all Germans, who still possessed old-fashioned gender roles. When the Germans do something, they do it thoroughly. That applies to work or pleasure. I was now to be the receptacle of their desires. Their attitude was cut and dried. "You are a lady-woman now! You receive pleasure from man!" they would say, their deep authoritative voices emanating from taut muscular bodies. They would whisper in my ear over and over, "Repeat after me: 'Schtick diene grosse schwanz in meine kleine futze.'" If they were drunk they'd grab your hand and put it on their crotch. They occasionally flashed tiny swastikas that they kept hidden in their pockets. They were thorough pleasure-seekers, intent on making the most of the joys of sex with their legendary ten-inchers.

I remember Klaus, major sodomy in his eyes, feeding me fresh ground sirloin in bed, insisting that I keep my Dior wig on. I bought expensive garter belts and shtrumpfhosen for him. I dressed like Irma La Douce. Wolfgang! My puppet. Mean eyes, deep voice, dirty socks, tight suits. You made me jack myself off when you were tired, then you'd watch. Sex beyond sex. Why did I ever leave you? Gerhard was the Fassbinder fantasy boy, baby-faced and deep voiced, Hunky Dory. We slow danced together to Abba.

In the morning, after the sun came up and we were all off work, we'd eat breakfast at Mau Mau, and then head over to the Kolisha, a fabulous bar, very rowdy. Brechtian, even. Everyone would be there: all the queens, strichers, and drag divas, the older ones in their mink coats and wigs with diamond earrings. The guys would be asking you how much money you made. Dangerous men. Real romantic.

One of the few native Germans who worked at Romy's was Rita Catastrophe. She was a pre-op transsexual who used to say funny things like, "For a clitoris I have a bratwurst." She was a little bit plump with long red hair, and a Marburger nose, named after the local queens' favorite plastic surgeon, Dr. Marburger. Rita was a part-time speed freak with a shady past from her previous job as a stripper. Romy was proud to have saved her from the sleazy five-dollar-blowjob-under-the-bar atmosphere of the strip clubs, where she used to do shows with elaborate theatrical themes like "Catherine the Great and Her Dildos." One show in particular stands out in its blatant and typically Germanic racism and bad taste. It was a women's prison scene in which a female inmate was whipped by a sadistic lady warden for having sex with a black man. Rita had testified against a local thug once and sent him to prison. When he got out, she said to me, "Beverly, I fear for my life." Not long after that she was found dead. Nobody was sure if he'd killed her, or if she'd been bumped off for not paying her bills (she had extravagant tastes but tended to ignore her debts), or if she'd just overdosed. I had a few clues I wanted to give to the police but Romy warned me not to talk to them, explaining that given the way the German police treat queens, they'd probably just implicate me. Berlin was a lawless world run by gangsters.

Back then a lot of the queens in Europe named themselves after perfumes: Zsa Zsa Dior, Ramona Ricci, Carol Cabochard. Carol had come from Paris with Romy and worked at Rolf Eden's, a naughty Eurotrash nightclub. Ricky Renee, the drag queen from the movie *Cabaret*, worked there. Carol was a cheap copy of Romy: loud, alcoholic, vulgar, and brazenly erotic. She wasn't what you'd call a blushing flower. She insisted on working in strip clubs because, as she said, "I need to feel my audience getting hard." While totally convincing as a beautiful woman, she was billed as "A boy made in Paris." Her gimmick was to strip down all the way, revealing not only her huge breasts but her huge dick.

One queen who didn't name herself after a perfume was Serge de Paris. He went on hormones shortly after Sugar and me, and became Zazie de Paris. She came with Romy from the Alcazar and was the choreographer for the show. It was because of Zazie's urgings that Sugar and I were hired; she'd seen our show at the Akademie der Künste and brought Romy to see us. She was very French and very flamboyant, with a dramatic, imposing face and prominent nose that she declined to have fixed. Her numbers in our show were always very artistic. Think Piaf. Think Lotte Lenya. She was more interested in art than glamour. I've always thought that's a better way to approach performance. I recently tracked her down (she tours constantly) and I'm hoping she sends me some of those fabulous German cabaret fantasy photographs of her with Claudia Schiffer that are the highlight of Karl Lagerfeld's recent coffee table book. She has had a sex change now and works as a theater actress. Her new name is Solange Dymanstein. Ain't it great to see someone flourish and grow, and become more and more fabulous with time?

During my stay in Berlin, Sugar and I really bonded doing hormones together. She was an army brat with perfect white teeth from a land-owning family in Gainesville, Florida, straight out of Tennessee Williams. They had great pedigree: Joan Fontaine was a relative. Sugar had lived in New York where she'd had an affair with Johnny Thunders of the New York Dolls, and had done her share of drugs. She'd also been a backup singer for Jobriath, a pretty boy Bowie clone, and had been on *Midnight Special* with Wolfman Jack wearing pink feathered platforms! Sugar was very attractive and very ambitious with an amazing talent for getting cast in shows, written about, and photographed. She was always in the center of things. It was almost frightening to watch her in her single-minded determination to get what she wanted. If a handsome man walked into a restaurant where she was eating she'd follow him into the bathroom and come out all smiles. Hibiscus used to say she "just dripped pussy juice." Her dog-in-heat grin was perfectly complemented by her beautiful blonde hair, worn in what was soon to become known as the Farrah Fawcett style. It wasn't at all surprising that she quickly became one of the greatest Marilyn Monroe impersonators of her time. Sugar taught me about makeup, hand movements, how to walk and talk and flirt. I'll always be grateful.

Living with Sugar in Berlin was wonderful. She'd come into my room every morning with hash. She did my hair weekly on our day off. We lived above the Scotch Club, a strip joint on Marburger Strasse of the Kudamm near Europa Center. I never really decorated except for one pinup of the newly discovered, very young Arnold Schwarzenegger. I'd lie in my room and read Genet's *Our Lady of the Flowers.*

I also got in a tiff with David Bowie in Berlin. It was 1975 and he was doing his *Station to Station* tour in his incarnation as the Thin White Duke. Everyone except me got tickets to see him at the Deutschland Halle. I was upset that after making history by coming out as bi a few years earlier he had just told the press he was straight. I felt that not only was it tacky to go back in the closet after coming out, but rather homophobic. Plus he'd used queer imagery to find a style and become famous, and now he was disowning the queers and transvestites, his biggest fans. It has come to light recently that the Ziggy Stardust image was created by a beautiful gay boy who lived in London, and Bowie definitely slept with boys.

After his performance, Bowie arrived at our club and posed with all of us for photographs. I think he'd instructed the photographer not to let us have any because she wouldn't and we almost choked her to death: "Give us those pictures!" He had a sweet voice like an English schoolboy. Real charming. He came back to the dressing room and was very interested in all us German cabaret people. Everyone wanted him to have a good time that night, and everyone was available for him: musclemen, little girls, you name it. It was decadent Berlin!

Romy said to me, "Beverly, don't talk to him about that fucking interview. Be nice to him, he's going to be our friend," but somehow it got out that I had a bone to pick. He said, "Oh, Beverly, never tell the press the truth, they'll twist it around." Really a stupid thing to say. Then he added, "Actually I'm changing my image. Time to butch it up." And he was! For his encore, he'd come out in jeans and mountain boots and a plaid shirt!

Back in the '70s, there were so many people who imitated Bowie, but Sugar and I always loved his wife, Angela. We thought she was like the hottest drag queen because she always had garter belts, petticoats, and strappy sandals, and was always going crazy. So I said, "I never wanted to be you, I wanted to be Angela." He replied, "Okay, Angela." I had just made my decision to go on hormones, and I was going for all out realness. His saying, "It's time to butch it up," seemed like he was almost challenging me a little bit, and I was challenging him a little bit back. Meanwhile, Romy was going, "Will you please not mess up my connection with David Bowie?!" He and Romy did hit it off and a picture of them kissing hit the international press a week later leading to a lot of tension amongst the pimps who were upset that Bowie didn't pay any attention to them.

The whole thrust of the evening with Bowie was commercialism. He said Lindsey Kemp, his mime teacher and an internationally famous gay performance artist, would never make money because he wasn't commercial enough. He signed his autographs "Bowie Incorporated" to announce the fact that he'd just taken control of his own corporation. Iggy Pop, who knew Sugar from New York, had come to the club with David and was very nice to us. He did make one rather upsetting remark in passing. Referring to the club, he said, "What a great idea to steal!" Sho' nuff, in David's *Boys Keep Swinging* video, he did a drag routine straight out of Chez Romy Haag, with Romy's signature moves from her encore song, "This Is My Life": tearing off his wig and smearing his lipstick across his face with a violent sweep of the arm. Although Bowie has always cannibalized other people for his own ends, his early work may be the greatest pop music ever written, and I believe he's one of the greatest singers of our time... serious moonlight/yuppie takeover/billion dollar corporate sellout notwithstanding.

Berlin was open, decadent, and free. My first day in Berlin I saw a seven foot tall Barbie doll hooker strutting down the street in broad daylight. I was so entranced I walked smack dab into a telephone poll. I loved Berlin! I loved all the clubs: the Trocadero, the Litsolampa, the Kolisha, the Tamara, all very queen friendly. I loved the hookers on Potsdamer Platz standing around in the snow wearing leather hot pants. I loved the opulent department stores, Warteim and KaDeWe, as seen on Robin Leach's *Lifestyles of the Rich and Famous*. I loved feeling like Sally Bowles, the '30s American cabaret singer character from Christopher Isherwood's *Berlin Stories* (played by Liza Minelli in *Cabaret*). I especially loved the fancy old world restaurant, the Winter Garden, with its Greta Garbo Room. I'd go there for afternoon coffee with the girls. We'd sit around for hours in our furs, dishing Romy and plotting to run away to Greece, dishing Amanda Lear for saying she was real, or just watching the snow fall. Everything was romantic to me, even the way my landlord had thugs kicking at our door when the rent was late.

It was the pantomime shows that finally got to me. I couldn't handle that plastic hofbrau, lip synch, commercial routine. "Now you make zee Midler number, now you make zee Shirley Bassey number." Pantomime is all about being either funny or beautiful, not about really connecting with people emotionally or intellectually. I had to get back to singing live with pianists, to using my own voice. I had to get back to San Francisco. Berlin was perfect in every way but that. That I had to come back for. Can you imagine having David Bowie in the audience and not being able to sing for him?! So after this heavenly, sexy, exhausting year, I left Berlin where I was safe, loved, well paid, and on my way to a sure career and probably marriage. I returned to America to risk near death as a transsexual, struggling for years to become a legitimate singer.

The Golden Age of Hustlers

Sugar and I were flown back to San Francisco by a desperate Hibiscus who wanted us to appear in his new extravaganza, *Femme Fatal: The Shocking Pink Life of Jane Champagne*, the Jayne Mansfield story. He had hooked up with George Cory who had written the classic "I Left My Heart in San Francisco," and gotten him to finance the show. George was a darling little ailing man who talked like Truman Capote and lived in a Pacific Heights townhouse. Hibiscus and Jack met him when they were working as call boys, and he bought them a 1956 Jaguar sedan, identical to the car Jayne Mansfield drove. When Hibiscus called us in Germany, he told us he had a theater and a producer with money. As it turned out, there was plenty of money for sets and costumes but no money for salaries. Sugar and I had to stay with Jack and Hibiscus, begging for tunafish sandwiches and iced coffee while we worked all day like theater serfs making headdresses in their kitchen.

The show featured tap dancing poodles and a Frederick's of Hollywood fashion show. I wore two pairs of super high-heeled bondage type '50s pumps from the Sex boutique of London where punk was being born, with a tight strapless dress made of solid rhinestone material that weighed what felt like forty pounds. The show flopped but I got great reviews. Hibiscus said, "They don't like us out here." I replied demurely, "Well, they like me." I'd worked with some of the best drag queens of my generation, but I was still the Eve Harrington, waiting for the star to break her leg.

Femme Fatal would probably have been a hit if we could have gotten a bodybuilder with whom Jack and Hibiscus had performed in Greece (he'd won the "Mr. Greece 1975" title) into the country to play the Mickey Haggerty role, but he was denied entry because of some minor criminal history. The show also had problems because it was ahead of its time. Its '50s camp sensibility would have gone over great in the New Wave era a few years later, but in '76 California was still into Mellow. We also did cocaine to celebrate after opening night and the press showed up the next night when we were crashing. Ooops. To make matters worse, by the mid '70s the gay community had turned away from drag, which was banned from the Gay Freedom parade, discos, and restaurants, even the Grubsteak on Polk Street! The Sisters of Perpetual Indulgence — queens who dressed up like nuns, frequently with Hibiscus-style face makeup — were constantly the subject of letters to the editor in the gay weekly papers. People were terrified that they were promoting "the wrong image" of homosexuals. The incredibly talented Sluts A Go Go performed more often at punk clubs than gay events. These were the clone years; drag was not again to be considered chic in San Francisco till the '90s.

Though the Angels were still around I couldn't really hang out with them anymore. They didn't quite know what to make of me, a rather brazen transsexual. It was all unspoken, so perhaps I was reading the situation incorrectly. It certainly seemed at the time though that the Angels disapproved of my transgendering. For one thing, my hormones were non-organic! The biological girls seemed especially unhappy. I hate the term "fag hag" for being demeaning, but it does describe a real dynamic with women who hang around gay men. They really love "their" gay boys for being cute and unattainable. Once I had breasts I was no longer the object of their sublimated desire, I was competition. They insisted on calling me Johnny. Being called by your female name is a big issue for transsexuals.

The Angels continued doing shows into the '80s, but were not quite as visible. They were busy dodging charges of welfare fraud and getting real jobs. Fortunately they had a romantic and spiritual side that made them less self-destructive and more enduring than many of the same generation, who ODed at a frightening rate. The Cockettes were still around too, but were all going their separate ways. Sylvester signed a contract with Fantasy Records, and was about to have his huge crossover disco hit "Mighty Real." Peter became a society pianist and founded the Art Deco Society to preserve Art Deco buildings. Over the years I've often dropped in on him at Les Trois, and sometimes late at night when he's in a good mood he'll play the old songs. For many, the Cockettes were one last pajama party/animal house/sorority bash before joining the real world, before becoming antique dealers, graphic designers, and teachers. The gold dappled world of the Deco queens was disappearing.

The Cockettes had pioneered a sort of shock therapy cabaret with blatant homosexuality, transsexuality, gender fuck, foul language, nudity, and high drag. Though they often worked with old Hollywood themes they fused them with a sexual anarchy that was radical even by today's standards. They were not only deconstructing

America's glamour myths from the '30s and '40s but redefining old school concepts of female impersonation. Rather than dressing up as a gay icon like Judy Garland or Barbra Streisand, or working some rich or suburban mainstream look, they created their own fantasy characters. Their drag was not about realness, but about fun and desire. They dealt with our culture's rigid gender roles in a playful manner, utterly subversive to what feminists call "the Patriarchy." Along with the Angels, the Warhol set, and Waters' crowd, they laid the groundwork for modern queer culture.

I never lost the dream of being a queen/star, which was permanently implanted in my head by the grandeur of what I had seen at the Palace Theater, reinforced by my stint at Romy Haag's. In retrospect, even the old school drag from that era looks rather appealing. All those men with fabulous wigs and full-on '60s housewife ensembles. Maybe I was more fascinated by drag than the others. To me, drag always looks beautiful, forbidden, and perhaps even blasphemous. It is my profession now, and like any other profession it requires experience, tenacity, and reinvention to succeed. I was prepared to make the commitment. I was a lifer.

Sugar went back to Berlin where her beauty was appreciated. Hibiscus returned to New York to do shows and hang out at Studio 54. He eventually met a rich older gay playboy and traveled the world. I never saw him again. In 1982 he died of a mysterious new disease referred to then as "gay cancer." Jack stayed behind in San Francisco for a time because he was making lots of money working as a hustler on Polk Street. He'd wear his fleece-lined denim jacket and stand in front of a neon sign that read "Hot Stuff." He introduced me to that scene, which I found rather seductive.

I became a streetwalker too, and hung out with the male hustlers on Polk Street. Streetwalking was almost considered politically correct by 1976. Margo St. James had formed C.O.Y.O.T.E. (Call Off Your Old Tired Ethics) to advocate for prostitutes' rights and legalizing prostitution. Transsexuals as well as lots of cute boy hustlers were all over Polk Street. 1976. Bicentennial Jimmy Carter America. Hotel California. Peter Frampton. Studly Dudly. Hustlers lined the streets at all hours trying to look like wholesome California boys with long feathered hair and super faded, so-tight-they-could-be-painted-on bellbottom jeans. This was what I call the Golden Age of Hustlers, 1976 to 1980, before AIDS and hard drugs like speed ravaged the streets. Polk Street was awash with New England college boys who'd show up on June 1st to work the circuit, Hollywood B-movie studs (I lived with one who had worked on *Pom Pom Girls for Satan*), and white trash jail boys with Southern accents, jail muscles, and little tattoos. The jail boys were really sexy; they weren't the twitchy, jittery drug casualties who showed up later. I lived in residence hotels and had passionate affairs with many Polk Street boys.

THE GOLDEN AGE OF HUSTLERS

An acid wash blue sky
hangs over Polk Street
from Post to Sutter
Bush to Geary
Hollywood Mike carves
his name on a
post at Cedar Alley
Real hustlers have
transsexual girlfriends
The smell of
nuggets and prospectors
drifts from the Grubsteak
Where I shared so

many cheeseburgers
with my hustler husbands
in the Golden Age of Hustlers

And the music was mellow
The Eagles and Fleetwood Mac
in cheap hotels
the Leland and the Cable Car
in tiny studios on Post and Larkin
like Genet or Isherwood love stories
we walk in the evening
and buy a joint
Billy the brunette TS
who passes so well
shouts from behind the
bar at the Black Rose
"What are you ashamed of?"
Voices return, "We all suck dick!"

Sweater queens singing
show tunes drunk all night
in the piano bars
I met Joey in the rain
Joey with his fabulous ass
made me proud
walking with him
a teenage pro from Dallas
so sexy until
the speed got him
so long ago in the
Golden Age of Hustlers

Eric was the king of
the street and looked
just like Paul Newman
as Fast Eddy in *The Hustler*
one lucky night
he bought a six-pack
and gave it to me
all night at the Cable Car
I saw the best bodies
of my generation
sold, bartered, and destroyed
by drugs and prostitution
But not all of them

Tommy and Thor
who looked so *Tom of Finland*
Tommy finally provided
me with the ultimate
porno dream fantasy come true
big buffed super hung
drug dealin' hustler
meets hot blond TS hooker
at 3 a.m. on speed
My secret life of sin
(Living well is my best revenge)
the queens hateful
but respectful
with their high nasal voices
the heinous runaway
teenage girls
the cops, the sweeps
the nights in jail

the attitude like bricks
that only we as a
race, a cult,
can walk through
because we like the sex

Gorgeous Vince the vice cop
with his big white teeth
paid to bust or have
sex with us
Vince was so hot
I wouldn't let him have me
unless he married me
the tension reaching
a breaking point
when he forced me
down on my hotel bed
and I screamed to
make him leave

There's love between hustlers
and TS's
there are no games and the
language is simple
and uneducated
Like Johnny T.
my lovely asthmatic
golden blonde
soccer ball bouncing
down the street
he came and
went between my place

and San Jose where he had
kids and sometimes
stayed with an old
black ex-pimp
who wanted to fuck him
Johnny like the rest
was a jail boy
"I ain't nobody's fuck boy!"
or "You got a couple more
years of booty"
I cried tears of love
on his chest at night
and he understood
my love and my deep sadness
he was my longest affair
and probably the only
man I ever loved
who ever really loved me

Toward the end
I met Michael Paul
who fit the mold so well
he called himself Danger Mouse
baby faced
bubble butt
butchy butchy
he had a tired Daddy
who kept him like a house cat
always had his laundry
done and his dinner
ready at seven o'clock
he came by for pot

and love in the afternoon
or late at night
on speed to suck my dick
say I had stars in my eyes
I hear he got out
and is a drug counselor
in Alaska

I now look back
through Pillars of Salt
at the shame
and the sadness
no one said life is fair
I see myself
so young
in the '70s
peasant blouses and skirts
my strappy high heel sandals
my YSL shades
Fiorucci bag
Farrah Fawcett hair or
all in black
like the girl on the
Lou Reed *Transformer*
album cover (who wasn't
Lou Reed by the way)
a girl whom the hustlers loved
I remember the
Golden Age of Hustlers

I had become a woman full time. No more fairy tales or fag hags, no more gay fantasies. I was in a new world now. This was the City of Night. Support your thug/pimps/punk-stud boyfriend. Fraternize with hard street hookin' transsexuals. Get busted and see the queens' tank at the Hall of Justice, 850 Bryant. Work it, Bitch. What alternative did I have? Get a real job and a real man? Sure, dream on.

San Jose Johnny: blonde, butch, sexy as hell, represented the dark new world I was entering. He was both athletic and tender and he remains truly dear to my heart. He had such a warm embrace. I melted. His face was hypnotic, his lips full and tempting, his voice so low and Daddy-like with a sidewalk cowboy accent. He was domineering in a way that was very easy for me to love. Only very handsome men can get away with it. I don't know if Johnny ever believed my stories; hustlers often live within the very narrow confines of street life. One day I got the opportunity to impress him by showing him an interview with Iggy Pop that had just come out in *Search & Destroy*, San Francisco's first punk zine. When asked, "Is Berlin decadent?" Iggy replied, "I love it. It's a fairyland. I met two American transvestites, Beverly and Sugar. Beverly is really tall, has beautiful carriage and great cheekbones." While Johnny wasn't as impressed as he would have been if, say, the Eagles or Captain & Tennille had mentioned me, he did seem somewhat amazed. Johnny, of course, left me crying. They all do. He went back to his wife and two adorable daughters: a real breeder. Transsexuality is trading away your respectability for sexual gratification. Or maybe I should say, was.

One night I was walking the street when a boy hooker gave me a quaalude and the terrible advice that if I wanted to make real money I should go downtown and cruise the hotels. I did, and lucky me, this was the night of the 1977 Valentine's Day queen sweep. It was infamous to the point where it merited an article in *F.I.M.* (*Female Impersonator* magazine). I was flat out propositioned by a policeman, entrapped. The arresting officer looked just like a *Charlie's Angels* villain in his winged collar shirt and leather sports coat. He took me to a room the vice squad keeps in the basement below the lobby of the St. Francis Hotel, where the walls are covered with Polaroid snapshots of streetwalkers. I began to cry and he told me to shut up, took my picture, and loaded me into the paddy wagon, which proceeded to drive around for two hours picking up more street trash.

Finally I ended up at the Hall of Justice at the holding tank. I was in there with these crazy men in a filthy terrifying environment. At last they transferred me to the queens' tank with thirty or so other pre-op transsexuals, some of whom I am still friendly with today! The next morning I woke up and experienced the camaraderie of prison life, which was like the queens' version of a women's prison film. The girls were flirting with the guards trying to get cigarettes, lining up to get their hormones from the jail doctor, and dancing on the tables to music from *The Don Ho Show*, which was on TV. There was one black queen with water balloon breasts who was screaming (there's always one queen who screams) about how the police report called her a woman. She wore the water balloons into court much to the delight of the prison populace. In court later that day, the handsome and well-dressed prosecuting attorney said to the judge, referring to me, "Your honor, this man is obviously sick." These were the bad old days. They weren't interested in helping us poor streetwalkers. They wanted a cut of the action. I was fined two hundred dollars.

A high school friend from my days at the Circle Star Theater was around Polk Street back then. Kenny had been playing Berger in *Hair* at the Orpheum, but by 1977 when the show finally closed, he gladly cut his hair, went New Wave, and began choreographing The Tubes. Kenny thought I was going a bit far with the hormones and he was right. Many doors closed professionally when I went pre-op. It's even hard to get female impersonator jobs if you're on hormones.

If the customers see real cleavage they can tell you're a TS and they freak out. They perceive it as cheating: you're not impersonating a woman; you are one. It's not a joke anymore. Forget television or musical theater. Forget *A Chorus Line, Jesus Christ Superstar, Cats,* etc. All you can do is underground movies or theater; even the rock'n'roll scene isn't very open. Kenny went on to choreograph the epic and indescribably kitschy *Xanadu,* as well as the underrated *One From The Heart,* and his breakthrough film, *Dirty Dancing.* Then he became a director, and did *Salsa, Newsies,* and Bette Midler's *Hocus Pocus.* Along the way, he choreographed Cher and Ann-Margret in Vegas, not to mention a Michael Jackson tour. Kenny and I have a funny relationship. When I think of us and our history, going back to the Circle Star, his success and my determination, I can't help but see us as modern day version of the Hudson Sisters from *Whatever Happened to Baby Jane?.*

Prisoners in Lace

In 1976, I started working as a stripper on Broadway in North
Beach. This is when I became known as Bambi, a name I chose
because it sounded very appropriate for the job. It was still the heyday
of topless burlesque, and I worked alongside stars like Taurus Rising,
Niki Knight, and Carol Doda. I started at a joint called the Roaring
'20s, but I was fired one afternoon after the owner chased me out
onto the street when I was topless. It was awful. After that incident,
of course, I learned not to call the boss an asshole, even if he was
one. Eventually I settled at the Galaxy. It was a goblin market where I
was like the girl in the red shoes who is condemned to dance forever
and ever. There was a mural on the wall of buxom blonde nude girls
frolicking in a forest with wolves. Looking back, it was a cozy setup.
No one was allowed to talk to me unless they bought me a drink. It

was like a line from that Dolly Parton song, "Single bars and single women, drinkin' beer an' amaretto, killin' time and swappin' jokes." At work we seduced and hustled men. It never stopped, day and night: businessmen, Hell's Angels, sailors, Army, Marines, and Air Force, too. The military men didn't have a lot of money, but they were the perks. I enjoyed hustling them. They were fun. It was nice to work as a woman instead of a female impersonator. What a relief not to do drag: no wigs or costumes, just lingerie and stockings. I did have to "tuck" to hide my dick.

A lot of the strippers were biker babes and official Hell's Angels wives with enormous bosoms, long hair, and big eyes. Their boyfriends would hang around often. These weren't dirty fat slobs; these were biker royalty. Tall, handsome, Conan the Barbarian-type road warriors. Together they looked like something out of a Frank Frazetta poster. The guys always wanted us to dance to heavy metal: Mötley Crüe, Ozzy Osbourne, Iron Maiden, AC/DC. I loved dancing to Foreigner's "Urgent" and "Girl on the Moon," ZZ Top's "Hot Legs," and Foghat's "Slow Ride." The bikers were leery of me till one day one of them kissed me on the knee and from then on they accepted me.

The Galaxy was fun but it also had a dark side. A lot of the girls who worked there did speed, coke, and heroin. Over the years the basement dressing room slowly evolved into a shooting gallery. Sad, sad, sad. Customers brought in huge bags of drugs for us, and the strippers had a way of becoming truly spectacular drug messes. Tex and Christina in particular. They'd come into work after three or four-day drug binges saying they were being chased by poltergeists, or drop their works right in front of the cops. Messy, messy, messy.

A lot of the girls were into black magic. Blanche, wife of notorious Satanist Anton LaVey, worked there at the time. He came to, of all things, the annual Christmas party. One day, Christina, in one of her more inspired drug rambles, began to expound on witchcraft and religion. She explained women's association with magic saying it was all about cycles of the moon, a feminine symbol. She observed that the Catholic Church used the constant symbolism of the mother and the son, never the daughter, and vilified non-virginal women. I'd heard all this before but then it really clicked for me. She went on to complain that everything was controlled by men, and it was all "done over the telephone." I often think of her remarks when musing about the state of the world. Actually, I feel that Jesus freed the slaves, and Christianity was about stopping people from selling their daughters in the marketplace. It's about the family, marriage, and fidelity. True love. And what's wrong with that? When I die I wanna go to Heaven. I want my harp, I want my wings, I want my whites, I want my cloud, and I want my Botticelli angel boys.

The Galaxy was a harem, and I was a spy in the house of love. I learned a lot of things about being a woman that I never would have otherwise by just reading or watching movies. The girls started out being wary of me because I was a transsexual. They were afraid I'd just use the place to turn tricks in. Eventually, by acting like a lady, they accepted me. Of course, they were allowed to act any way they wanted. They would endlessly discuss their periods and mood swings. There was nothing like PMS Night — the first or fifteenth of every month — when Miss Carol, the Deadhead girl who wore satin hot pants, would come in, slam her fist on the table, and scream, "Don't anybody fuck with me tonight!"

LADY BOY STRIPPER FOR THE U.S. MILITARY

I was a stripper at the Galaxy
on Broadway in North Beach
Ten years, from '76 to '86
I started at the Roaring '20s club
but got fired for calling the owner an asshole

He chased me out onto the street topless
in the middle of the afternoon
The Galaxy was sort of
shabby, sparse, and dark
I worked with my dick tucked
really tight between my legs
I wasn't supposed to date customers
because they might find out
I wasn't really female

We danced to the jukebox
and sat and drank with the men
I danced to hard rock
The Galaxy was unique
it was the only bar on Broadway where
you could really get drunk with a stripper
My boss, Herbie "the Chinaman"
loved my long legs
and told me to keep my knees together
when I walked on stage
I was a walker
I tried not to date the clients
but after I got my tits done
well, things just happened
mainly with the military guys
I can't remember any of their names
but I do remember faces, bodies
and certain sexual highlights
Most of the time I just teased and tempted but...
sometimes over the years I gave in

One day in particular
I took a big handsome young sailor
backstage to smoke a joint
We did things like that at the Galaxy
but no one ever turned a trick on the premises
I started to go down on his ten-inch dick
He stood me up then sat down
pulled down my G-string
and went down on me!
Lots of the military men were hip to TS's
because of the Philippines
He told me he knew she-males in L.A.
We dated for about two years, when he was in town
They came and went…
on the Enterprise, the Kitty Hawk, the Kansas
I met a shy tall blond sailor with good muscles
who said heavy metal was full of prophesy
we sunbathed on the roof
of the Cable Car hotel near Polk Street
I took a Navy Seal to my room
at the Skyway across the street from the Galaxy
Seals are so exquisite
I met a Southern gentleman petty officer
who wanted a long relationship
but I left him on New Year's Eve
to do speed with a cute brunette

I met a Drill Sergeant I'll never forget
I walked on his chest
downstairs in the dressing room
in my high heels
and verbally abused him

it was wonderful
I met another Seal one night
on Polk Street at Travelers
but stupidly blew it
by drinking too much scotch
I met this Tom Cruise lookalike
army guy back at the Galaxy
He was wearing a Don Johnson sports coat
This was the '80s
with a black t-shirt
he was dating Kimberly
this underage beauty I worked with
but she had gotten the clap or something
so I got him
I rarely let anyone actually fuck me
but I let him, three times that night
It was so wonderful until
he returned to the bar the next morning
and complained to Herbie
that I was not a real woman
Herbie just laughed

Passing was always touch and go
If anyone asked
Is that a change, a tranny, a ladyboy?
Deadhead Carol said,
"No, she's just German"
On occasion, whole ships
would sabotage me
the Kittyhawk was in port
I was very cautious
but after a while the cutest stud

took me home and fucked me
the next day everybody knew
They stopped buying me drinks
they stopped tipping me
and sat with the other girls
one of whom was Little Joy
who was also a transsexual
but they didn't know

When Little Joy came to work with us
everyone favored her over me
she was so petite and real,
with her huge helpless eyes,
natural blonde hair and full hips
instead of killing myself
as any common aging queen would have done
I got flawless breast implants and from then on
me and the sailors and Little Joy got on just fine
Little Joy got very involved with speed and bikers
she disappeared into the Everglades of Florida
and hasn't been heard from since

Goodbye, Little Joy, wherever you are
Once this officer with the most unbelievable ass
surprised me by rolling over
and offering it up to me
Well, I took it and took it and took it
I still dream of seeing him again
I remember the boys on the Enterprise
They used to say
"Beam me up, Scotty!"
One night a gang of marines

strolled in late, looking mean
They had just gotten in a big fight
somewhere on Battery Street
Herbie served them
big strong Long Island Iced Teas
they slowly got relaxed and real friendly
They started coming two or three times a week
I sat on the cutest one's lap all night
and flirted and giggled
and soon I was so in love
I didn't know what to do
So I finally took him up to the Skyway hotel
and told him my secret
He was very bewildered
I gave him head sadly
and they never came back

I learned a lot about men
subtle things, telepathic things
I dream about men sometimes
muscular men in dark midnight gardens
in warm lagoons
the soft sound of the water rippling
large bodies, slowly moving towards me
with enormous hard-ons,
deep murmuring voices, diving, swimming
it's the army, the sailors, my boys, my men

Once this mysterious bald man
with dark glasses came in
(very Helmut Newton)
he worked for Shell Oil

he ordered champagne
and started tipping me hundreds
a hundred when I danced
a hundred at the end of the shift
I was so high on champagne
I took him to my hotel and made more
it was $800 total
things like that happened at the Galaxy
when the big money came I usually got it
another older man
became a regular
spending thousands at a time
on golden credit cards
It was like something from
the Moulin Rouge, Paris 1890
champagne bottles everywhere
hundred dollar bills
we'd just swirl around this kind old toad
talking baby talk
it must have been like that
in the Barbary Coast days
the Gold Rush honkytonks
"We nailed him to the cross,"
Herbie would say

It sometimes seemed the place was going broke
it was so often empty
people thought we were nuts
sitting around this empty bar
and it was strange
this vacant boring brothel space
the waiting

we were the ultimate spider women
weaving silver gossamer webs
to catch our victims

The day I started at the Galaxy I met Gloria, a rich cross-dressing male lawyer. She set me up in a spacious Russian Hill highrise apartment with a pool and a breathtaking view of the bay. She paid for electrolysis, hair appointments, long distance calls to Berlin, my punk wardrobe, my vintage wardrobe, my *Eyes of Laura Mars* '70s fashion model wardrobe, endless restaurant dinners and cocaine parties. I had hand-beaded gowns made. I got my tits done. I was even allowed to have my boyfriends stay with me. It was heavenly. What a set-up, holy cow, they'd never believe.

What did Gloria want in return? A lot of people took it for granted that I was sleeping with her, which I wasn't. I'm not that kind of girl. Gloria just wanted someone to dress up with; our relationship was very mother/daughter. She looked sort of like R. Crumb or the Nutty Professor in drag. She was six feet tall and teetered around on six-inch heels, had an enormous nose, and was constantly wheezing. Once you got past her somewhat disconcerting appearance she was very likable: gentle, friendly, and also very classy. She was from old San Francisco money, so naturally we had season opera tickets, and could go into Vanessi's or Swiss Louie's and be well received.

I really owe my current career to her. She heard me singing Helen Morgan songs in soprano as she drove me home one night and offered to pay for opera lessons. A little French man came to the door every Tuesday morning for two years to train me in bel canto. Like everything in my life at that time, though, Gloria had a dark side. She liked drugs and constantly drank scotch to the point where it damaged her health. She liked danger, and eventually got in with the wrong sort of hustlers. Why do I always attract these people?

Bambi with V.S.

Roberta Shreds

Around this time, 1977, punk exploded at the Mabuhay Gardens two doors up Broadway from the Galaxy. The guy who booked the club, Dirk Dirksen, started presenting new bands from Britain, New York, and L.A. I'd been hearing about this scene since '74 in Manhattan when Tomata's best friend, Guerilla Rose, turned to me and said, "Da only ting happenin' in dis town is da Ramones." In Berlin I'd been an avid reader of the weekly British rock newspapers, *N.M.E.*, *Melody Maker*, and *Sounds*, in which I learned more about the Ramones and other new punk bands like Blondie. When my roommate Ginger (with whom I lived before I met Gloria) showed me a picture of The Clash, Paul Simonon's working class, pouty yet butch, big-eyed, ultra-British beauty won me for punk rock forever.

Many people who'd been part of the whole '60s counterculture couldn't relate to punk at all, with its highly theatrical artifice and violence. They didn't realize that there were a lot of very creative people in the new punk scene, including my old pal Tomata, who'd become lead singer of a legendary L.A. band The Screamers. They had great songs: "I'm Going Steady with Twiggy," "Cholo," "Peer Pressure." The Screamers' logo (a black and white caricature of Tomata's face screaming in rage with his hair on end) is still used by ACT-UP in its posters. Far from being the teenage hooligans many people imagined them to be, the original punk scene in San Francisco was composed of trendy art school students, talented musicians, fashion designers, dissident intellectuals (lots of Dada and deconstruction points-of-view), and an amazing number of trust fund babies. That's usually how it works: when there's a new trend, the rich kids get there first. Anyway, they were stimulating company.

One night I went to see The Avengers. The lead singer, Penelope Houston, had blue hair and had painted her throat to look like it had been slashed. Hardly anyone was there. Two weeks before, one of the TV news shows had run a twenty-minute piece on punk rock because the Sex Pistols had hit number one on the U.K. charts with "God Save The Queen." A scene popped up out of nowhere, and I became a permanent fixture at local punk shows. I'd be there in pink stretch pants, a mohair sweater, with a patent leather '50s purse, and patent leather spike heels. The punk boys couldn't get enough of me. Punk was my last dream world. It was so… European, so New York junkie. Johnny Thunders once tried to get me to cop and go to a cheap hotel to do heroin with him! I was constantly shopping. Punk diva and author Jennifer Blowdryer used to say that you could go to Europe for the price of my Charles Jourdan heels. She was always traveling and I was always buying shoes. It was worth it, though, because those shoes found me the love of my life, Baba.

BABA

Baba black sheep have you any wool
Yes sir, yes sir, three bags full
Baba wasn't a hustler
he was a Latin baby punk star
from Chula Vista
Teen Beat dreamy, drummer for the Zeros
Tried to pick me up at the Mab
When he was sixteen
Hmmm Ahhh
I told him to come back later
He did, at eighteen
Baba loved my French disco heels, my Dior perfume
Grew tall dark and handsome, strong and silent
Orlando Cepeda baseball cards
My mother would have loved him!

Black denims and cholo boots
Boy Scout shirt and brown beret
Shark dancing to the New York Dolls,
Delightful!
Big brown eyes, like the prince in
Walt Disney's *Sleeping Beauty*
He read the *Basketball Diaries*
He was always shooting baskets
With punk rock tomboy girls

Sleeping in on rainy days
listening to Eno sing "Spider and I"
relishing every second
'cause I knew all this was way too good

to last long
he talked like a child and called me Mom
Just once I came on his stomach
and he got up and went to church

On Valentine's Day he gave me taboo kisses
like Sabu in *Black Narcissus*
bought me flowers
took me to the porno films
like De Niro took Cybill Shepherd
in *Taxi Driver*
The happiest night of my life
sex like See's Candies
in a red velvet heart-shaped box
Tomata introduced us
and I like to think of us as having a real place
in rock history
in our Bambi's dreamhouse apartment
we were like the punk rock Lucy and Ricky
"Honey! I'm home from the Clash concert."
He was always asking, "Can we have a dog?"
Can we have a dog?
I had a Dilaudid prescription so we could be
high class pharmaceutical junkies
I cling to memories of long evenings
at home, him saying to me
with his Elvis lips
"Tell me some of your stories, I like your stories"
I'd order a Tomasso's pizza, play Edith Piaf
and tell him about the old Fillmore, the Summer of Love,
Berlin, New York, Provincetown,
Iggy, John Waters, Cookie Mueller

they were bedtime for Baba stories
he'd listen, his eyes as big as saucers, sparkling
like a Japanese comic book hero
like a Margaret Keane painting

His dick like a hero, like a prince, like a husband
Goldilocks would have said
"Not too big, not too small, just right"
really it was too big, which was just right
I love you, I love you
I just love you

Long after he left me
in ugly '87
I saw him at the I Beam
I dressed up real sassy
like a rock wife
we talked and flirted and drank too much
shooting baskets with maraschino cherries
when he blew me off at the end of the night
it just went snap, it just went snap,
my life went snap
I hit him hard
on the jaw, with a closed fist
I wanted to show him what girls and cars
were really all about
I never hit anyone before
I guess I needed to ritually return
the years of pain endured
when he casually, quietly
strolled out of my life

Baba is married now and has a daughter
I hear he's put on weight
I should probably leave well enough alone
But...

Baba was the drummer for The Zeros, who had a punk rock hit with their song, "Wimp." Amazingly enough, they started out as protégés of Tomata's band, The Screamers, who often acted as their legal chaperones so they could go on tour (they were all underaged). Baba's big number on stage was an instrumental version of "Road Runner", not Jonathan Richman's song but the cartoon version as done by Mitch Ryder and the Detroit Wheels, accented by Baba saying, "Beep Beep," on the break. One night at the old Back Door when the Zeros were playing their cover of "Little Latin Lupe Lu," they let me jump up and go-go dance for them. I was wearing a red spandex, backless, long sleeve mini-dress that was years ahead of its time. I also introduced the band at the Pauley Ballroom on the U.C. Berkeley campus in a flesh-colored soufflé (transparent mesh) dress covered in sequined orchids appliqués and dripping in orchid turkey boas. That night I had consumed a ton of MDA and started rushing so heavily I ascended upwards. The band was blaring, the sequined orchids were exploding, my jaw was shaking out of control. Then it passed and I felt great. Later I followed Baba down a long spiral staircase like in so many dreams I'd had, only it wasn't a dream.

Baba had been staying with me for a while when I realized that there was a rather sinister social dynamic going on. The punkettes were all saying that Baba was sleeping on my couch. He was straight. People are forever thinking that I sleep with gay guys, and that a straight man would never in a million years be attracted to me. Wrong. Wrong. Wrong. Once I started hormones it was basically over between me and gay men. No more hanging out with the gay

Marines at the Barracks on Folsom Street. After hearing the rumors, I had a decision to make. Should I go public? I didn't want people thinking that I was some old queen supporting him just to bask in his presence. He was willingly in my bed! I told my friend Ginger to print the truth in her zine, *Punk Globe*. Baba moved out the week after the issue was printed. For all the anarchy filtering through the scene, to be thought of as homosexual was still a stigma for punks.

Losing Baba was like being left at the altar. Thinking about him can still make me howling-at-the-moon crazy. A great loss like that can either destroy you or force you to maturity. To save myself, I had to stop being a spoiled princess, abandon my chronic melancholia, and grow up. But all that emotion is still there somewhere driving me onward. He'll always be my sweet inspiration.

I joined the all-girl punk band VS. (pronounced "versus") in 1980, replacing a girl named Heidi. The other girls were Crayola and Olga. We wore lots of vinyl and dressed like Diana Rigg from *The Avengers*. We did a cover of "Paint It Black" but our big song was "Leather Complex." I used to really scream my head off. They had this running gag that they were in, something called Fashion Patrol, and they'd scream and point out fashion violations like, "Versus Fashion Patrol, you're wearing BEIGE!" We opened for X, Dead Kennedys, and Jayne County & The Electric Chairs among others. The band would come out and scream, "This is bondage rock."

After a show, we'd snort tons of Peruvian flake cocaine. I have no happy memories of cocaine. My skin crawls when I think of it. I'm rather high strung and nervous by nature. While the coke did make me feel good for a little while, it generally made me too paranoid for the experience to really be enjoyable. Why did I continue to do drugs when I didn't enjoy them? Good question. Back then cocaine hadn't been popular long enough for everyone to see all the terrible damage it eventually can do.

I had a problem with VS. in that I felt boxed in by the leather bitch image. Chrissie Hynde is one of the few who ever pulled that off with style. I never really got into the trashiness that was so chic on that scene. I'd be on stage wearing a brand new Swanky Modes dress from London, tight red spandex with a slash across the front, hemmed up, and I'd have just had my hair done, and I'd say stuff like, "This is I. Magnin's rock!" Olga hated that. They wanted me to be a big tall blonde Teutonic dominatrix, while I wanted to be a witty singing Jerry Hall or Patti Hansen.

Not to be outdone, Rodney from the Angels of Light surfaced as a punk diva with his new band, the Wasp Women. The ensemble made a hilarious punk statement with their beehive hairdos, tight black vinyl dresses, and water balloon breasts that shook when they danced. They had a terrific song, "You Stupid Queen, You Act Like A Machine." He was also starring in *Holy Cow* with the Angels, which was wowing people at Project Artaud.

The other boyfriend I had at the time was English. I first laid eyes on six foot tall, handsome as sin, eighteen-year-old Freddy in front of the Mab. He was wearing full on black leather, good smelling English leather. He had an incredible ass. His older brother was one of the original punk rockers and had arranged for him to stay with Vale, publisher of *Search & Destroy*, and later RE/Search. He was from south London where he'd grown up in a council house. He was a real tough guy, like a British boy's school bully, or the Daniel Day Lewis character in *My Beautiful Launderette*. His accent changed depending on his outfit, from Cockney if he was dressed down, to upper crust when he was dressed like a "toff." He possessed a rockabilly/ska, male model type, centerfold beauty. I let Freddy stay with me for what was supposed to be a short while; Baba was scheduled to move in at the end of the month. When the time came to send Freddy packing, I was faced with a terrible decision: which boy do I let stay with me? Freddy won.

Why did I choose Freddy? Maybe it was because he had the

sweetest cum I've ever tasted. Well, he was a real Casanova. He knew all about blowing in your ear, and kissing you on the neck, and gently feathering your nipples then biting them. Incredible. Our love life consisted of my blowing him. He was always the initiator. Usually once in the morning after we'd showered, and once at night. Only on one occasion did he blow me. I had dragged our mattress off the bed and in front of the TV in the hopes of refocusing his attention on me and our anticipated pleasures. Cute. Our relationship was tempestuous, lots of rough housing, lots of fighting, lots of one-upmanship. I loved that. I also loved walking arm in arm with him in public.

Freddy had a series of pretty boy jobs, gofer at Sh-Boom's (a punk boutique), doorman at the Mab and the Deaf Club, but he was basically a gigolo. He could never stay in a band because he'd get all the girls and the other guys would get jealous. He did at one point become a roadie for The Clash (for a short while), and was pictured with them in *Rolling Stone* the night they dedicated "Stay Free" to him. After the show we went to their hotel room, which was strewn with books they'd bought at City Lights bookstore. The bass player later married local diva Pearl E. Gates. I juggled Freddy and Baba, my two punk paramours for years.

Freddy and I finally broke up when he got too heavily involved with drugs. We'd always been around amphetamines and pot. Our first night together we stayed up all night on speed he'd copped from a member of Flipper. Later on though, Freddy got involved with heroin and an East Bay dealer's moll named Clover. He left me for her to become a big time gangster. The day he packed up to go, I cried and shrieked. The experience was made all the more surrealistically painful by my cruel neighbors, a middle-aged couple, who always thought I was too loud. I could hear them mocking me by imitating my wails through the walls. Boo Hoo Hoo. He showed up again a few months later after having had a bullet removed from his back.

He arrived during a sleepover party Baba and I were having for all of Baba's little friends. Freddy was so nasty I had to physically throw him out.

The bad side of Freddy was something I had to eventually accept. However, when we were in love, life was a dream. I didn't really see anyone but him. I was up above in Patti Smith's land of love, with Frederick. He was so charming that we were accepted by all the youngest, artsiest punksters. The Avengers and The Dils loved Freddy, but I treasured our time alone. Getting him on the bed. Getting him horny. Freddy near my face. Purring to him. How could he be only eighteen and so tall? When we were lying down we could stretch out and still be toe to toe and eye to eye. His body was almost voluptuous for a man. He had curves. His ass was a little too big, which was very arousing. I remember buying brand new comforters, sheets and pillowcases from Macy's, very French provincial, making things all the more honeymoon-like. Pillow talk in a thick English accent is a real aphrodisiac. He was a master at foreplay. He cradled me and bent me in different directions, embracing me and bending me slightly back. Licking my ears and neck, breathing hot air down my ear. He was like a vampire, dark and hungry, gothic before I'd ever heard the word. Freddy's fascination with the neck was his love secret. He was a master at titillating this so often overlooked erogenous zone.

Freddy was a king bee, and I was a red, red rose in full bloom. He was Heathcliff to my Jane Eyre. He was The Clash to my Blondie. The early punk years were ridiculously romantic times. We were struggling kids living in tiny studio apartments, and love was the only reasonably priced entertainment left in America. We held hands in the street; we kissed in taxicabs. I knew how to suck him off like a fag though I looked like a woman. It was best in the morning. The sun streaming through the drapes. He liked to straddle me with his hands on the headboard, and buck away like a stallion while I opened my mouth and breathed through my nose, to give his dick access to the deepest reaches of my throat. I moved the very back of my tongue sideways, back and forth, quickly. His cum was so sweet.

FREDDY

Like Alfie he used his cold Cockney charm
to the hilt
ska dancing in his leathers and brothel creepers
his skinny ties and drape jackets
that I bought him
Freddy made love like
a professional gigolo
the punk girls called him "Gigs"
he liked me to dress like Modesty Blaise
Listening to "Young Americans" on the jukebox
at the Palms Cafe
We smoked Dunhill Reds
we wore day-glo mohair sweaters
we were so chic
in those Vivienne Westwood days
Madness, the Specials, X-Ray Spex
he was always writing poetry
and once read with Burroughs
the poem was "Lift Up Your Skirts"
a shady character
cunning and vain
our love affair was like a war
of one-upmanship
he got a motorcycle
I got my tits
he slept with Pearl E. Gates

I slept with Danny Avenger
his best friend
we did pearlescent
Peruvian flake cocaine
and wrote film scripts to star in
me as the Countess Bathory
us as upper echelon Nazis of the master race
he was fascinated by blood
began reading the Marquis de Sade
after he got into bodybuilding
he would never let me touch him
egoiste, egoiste, egoiste
finally heroin made an absolute mess of Freddy
and he was deported
but I'll always brag about him
tall and very good looking
he made me tingle
and ripple with pleasure like Lady Chatterley
I hear he's now married in Japan
and a video performance artist
I swore I saw him in the Jean-Claude Van Damme film
Blood Sport
Freddy was an Aries
I am a Libra
we had this Mars and Venus
God of war, goddess of love thing
he wore the first pair of Doc Martens
in San Francisco
Freddy was a user
a gigolo, a heel
and a flim flam man
he was unworthy of me

but without a hurt
the heart is hollow

Honestly, regardless of how much hot sex with trade you have, when you get into a real relationship, sex becomes making love. It didn't last long enough with these boys to take them for granted. These relationships existed on a higher plane than any size-queen/muscle/sailor fantasy I have lived out. Unlike my only previous love, San Jose Johnny from the Polk Street scene, these two weren't street; they weren't trash. They were artists. True love has been the greatest theme in western art, and when you come right down to it, love is pretty rare. I feel pretty lucky to have been able to experience that Bootsy Collins Astral Love Groove. Baba and Freddy weren't queenfuckers. It took some pretty hard work to capture them. As much as I tend to see myself as a victim of these two Casanovas, I also congratulate myself on having seduced two incredible young men. Punk was a youth cult and for me, at twenty-eight, to have ensnared two eighteen-year-olds was one hell of an achievement, something characteristic of a real she-wolf. One thing about having tasted true love, having experienced that cloudy weightlessness, is that I will crave it viciously, savagely, for the rest of my life.

Classic musclemen have always been a sexual turn-on, but the rock'n'roll boys are the ones to fall in love with. They're not like hustlers or johns, or even the military. They worship pussy; they aren't queen fuckers. During the punk era they became a big challenge: I was drawn to them like a moth to a flame. Unfortunately, they tend to be somewhat unattainable. As Terri La Tour, drag diva extraordinaire of London, used to say, "The most we can hope for is an affair." For all its faux androgyny, rock and roll is one of the stalwart bastions of stone cold hetero-ness. Anais Nin once said that transvestites and transsexuals are guerrillas in the battle of the sexes, and I've experienced the front lines of this battle. Bayonets, muddy boots, and hair appointments.

Rock and roll is so incredibly sexual. It's the one way in our society that straight men can really flaunt their sensuality. Actors may get applause, but rock stars get screams. The girl who gets to go home with the love object of five thousand crazed fans is in for a big ego rush. That may be part of the attraction, but not all of it. I'm not a groupie; I'm actually part of the music community. Although there's no denying an element of seeking approval and acceptance in these conquests, they're also just a way of tagging someone, of cementing a relationship. Often once is enough.

Sexually I played the game and was very submissive. I never got fucked though, because they were afraid of my pelvic area. So mainly I just got to suck a lot of real hot straight rock'n'roll dick. But I never lost my head, even when I was giving head. Real rock'n'roll guys are the golden sons of the universe. God's gift. They bestow blessing when they reveal their nakedness. I'm not being sarcastic, it's true and you know it! I've slept with very few of these guys as I don't have an almighty vagina. I'm willing to bow down but not all the way over. I'm not about to make a blood sacrifice of my genitals on a stone altar of heterosexuality. I made my decision not to be male but she-male. I totally objectify those men as fabulous holy sex objects and they hate me for it. And they love me for it.

One of my favorites was a bass player who was my age. The only real bonafide rock legend of my career. Drop dead gorgeous. Classic English looks, dark hair, light skin, dark eyes. He was the pinup boy of the group. He had a black belt in karate and a degree in physics. A very sexual nature. The group recently held their twenty-year anniversary comeback tour. There's a rumor that he's Luis Bunuel's son. Our night of love... There I was at The Stone, standing by the stage, wearing black Levi's and a low-cut tank top. The guitar player was playing to me staring down my cleavage. Summoned backstage to dance for one of their best tunes. Every night they had a girl strip for that song as the finale. After I took off my jeans they discovered I was a transsexual because I wasn't tucked that night. I wasn't expecting to be seen in my undies. There was a lot of competition backstage. There were even some thirteen-year-old girls hanging around. After some negotiations, I bamboozled my way back to the hotel with him in his chauffeured car. There were groupies waiting outside the hotel. In his hotel, I looked for a razorblade because I was beginning to show stubble. It was sort of like the scene from *Sweet Charity* where she goes home with the Italian movie star and sings, "If they could see me now." He wanted to investigate; he was adventurous. He was one of few punk rocker dudes who sucked my dick. That experience was as close as I've ever come to being in a romance comicbook story. Fantasy and reality collided at that moment. Sigh.

Then there was a drummer that I just had to have. I'm ashamed to admit it, but I gave him money. I was like a kid in a candy store. He was really, really cute and blonde and wore lots and lots and lots of black. Everybody liked him. He was from Canada and his dad was a Royal Canadian Mountie.

Another drummer I adored wins the Punk Rock Male Spokesmodel Category Award for all time. He had the Face of Punk. When he played drums he sweated buckets. He played harder than anybody. He was mostly monogamous with his girlfriend. One day, he came to the door looking for Freddy, who was out but I assured him he was welcome to wait. I happened to be wearing my Bob Mackie amethyst silk satin and lace teddy, and matching flowing robe with Guenevere sleeves that hung all the way to the floor, accompanied by matching amethyst Charles Jourdan pumps with leather Chinese fans on the toe. Magically, his pants came down. I was born on the Scorpio cusp, and my energy is like an undertow. I was irresistible. Imagine his pants spontaneously unbuttoning at my penetrating glance. It may have helped that we were cheating on each of our live-in lovers. Some sexual experiences have religious significance. This particular blowjob is one of those. It was like Marilyn Monroe in *The Seven Year Itch* when she walks into Tom Ewell's fantasy in a skintight sequined tiger evening gown looking scornful, and says, "I love Rachmaninoff. It shakes me, it quakes me, it makes me feel goose pimply all over." Poor adorable drummer boy. He got a gig touring with Joan Jett and ended up strung out on heroin. He lost his job two weeks before "I Love Rock 'n Roll" hit number one. Talk about dreams that fall through your fingers. I'm happy to report he now lives in Sweden and works in a health food store.

Then there was the lead guitarist I enjoyed at a kegger party in a warehouse. I had just had my tits done. Joey was a big burly, charmingly chunky guy. The other boys in his band were always blonde love dolls. He fixated on me and was very attentive. He had a fabulously sexy deep voice. The band gave me a ride home from the party in their van. I sat on his lap. He was so big I felt like a little girl, and we made out intensely as the van bounced along.

Another time, I was coming home from a party with a different lead guitarist as the sun came up, and he was wearing a sharkskin suit on his tall (6'4"), lanky, Jimmy Stewart-like frame. He had lost his car and ended up staying with me at my hotel. He looks a little like Howdy Doody, and in my book, that's a compliment. I love being with someone who's bigger than me, and I love the strong silent type.

I first met this fabulous drummer at the legendary Ramones' first gig in San Francisco at the Savoy Tivoli. I went backstage after the show, and bumped into none other than Miss Titty, a notorious, snaggle-toothed, SSI queen, angel dust dealer, and Vietnam vet. I knew her because she'd been in the Angels of Light but she had gone noticeably downhill since then. She'd given Dee Dee some angel dust, and he was just sitting there repeating, "I'm in the oooozone." I kept thinking, How dare she corrupt this darling boy in such a manner... Disgraceful! Anyway, that's where I met another fabulous drummer. He drove an old Cadillac, always wore vintage '60s suits, and was a real playboy. He'd talk about hot and cold running blondes, like something from a Matt Helm movie. He was a real Good Time Charlie, a Mabuhay regular. One sloshy night after a big party we ended up together at my hotel. Well... after I got my tits done, it seemed they all had to have me.

A different drummer I knew from around the scene but had never connected with, until one night when I walked into a party with Freddy and was pulled into the master bedroom where we consummated our passion amidst the vintage thrift store vinyl coats and jackets. We slept together on a steady basis till one morning he asked for fifty dollars for the privilege of continuing to see him. Being a punk gigolo takes a little more finesse than that, so I sent him packing. He was totally my type: 6'3", handsome, slender, strong and silent. We were a great match. I give great head and he had a big ole honkin' dick. Too bad it had to end.

Everyone always looked forward to seeing the L.A. bands when they came to the Mab: the Go Gos, the Screamers, the Bags, X, the Germs, the Alleycats. One time, I got in a van after the show with the band and Miss Gerber. Gerber was a teeny tiny L.A. punk rock chick with teeny tiny cowboy boots who was a major instigator of punk riots in front of the Roxie in '78. We went off to some party somewhere, and they rolled a yard-long spliff with rag weed. It was a real giggly high, and I did it on the couch in the living room with one of those L.A. guitar boys. He was just so sweet and butch, with his dark hair and pasty drug addict complexion.

In those days I was living as a woman. When I'm involved with straight rockers that's generally what happens. There weren't a lot of hipster queens around in those days. Sure, there were a few drag queens here and there, but by this time I was in another world from them. I was playing the overtly sexual part of the Other Woman, who won't go away.

The Clash were so friendly when they were in town, but the rest of the English punk stars were not as inviting. So I'd call their hotels and pretend to be famous people. I called Gary Numan backstage at The Warfield and told his manager I was Charlotte Rampling. I said I knew him from Tubeway Army, could I have a backstage pass? I got into the show in a box seat but didn't get backstage. A year later I called Bauhaus backstage at Wolfgang's, and the same manager answered the phone so I was invited to their hotel. I drank all night with them and some teenage girls, then told them it was a hoax and left. I called up Bryan Ferry and he was super nice, and so was his wife Lucy. I called The Specials and told them I was Jerry Hall, and that I was standing outside across town in a phone booth in a mink coat and a garter belt, and tried to get them to come pick me up.

My apartment was a party house and a hangout for a lot of the local punk bands. They would drop by and watch television or whatever. Steve Jones of the Sex Pistols used to come over with the Avengers whose album he was producing. The Sex Pistols! I vividly recall Sid on stage at the Mabuhay when they came to town in '78, lumbering around with Alice Bag, a wonderful girl. He had on the gay guys fisting t-shirt. He was very tall, pretty, and innocent looking without the fake blood and goofy face for the camera. Anyway, Steve Jones had just been swimming in my pool when the news about Sid stabbing Nancy came over the radio. He said it was all her fault.

One day a miracle occurred. Siouxsie Sioux, who was staying with a friend of my friend Ginger Coyote, walked into The Galaxy with her entourage. She was wearing full-on Siouxsie hair and makeup, and full-on leather regalia. Not many people realize how tall she is — as tall as I am, six foot three in heels. She must be one of the most beautiful women of our generation: her face has that very English beauty that Evelyn Waugh would have said made her resemble "a heroine out of Renaissance tragedy." She danced on stage to Sinatra, then Jimi Hendrix. Later we walked down to

Earl's, a nearby New Wave disco on Battery Street, together. As we passed the Transamerica Pyramid with the full moon behind it she really looked like a rock and roll Cleopatra. At the door to the club they asked her if she was an impersonator! Inside as people began crowding in on her she threw a glass against a wall, which shattered right near some girl's head. Everyone backed off. They started playing her music and she said, "Take it off." When Roxy Music's "Both Ends Burning" came on, I said, "Siouxsie Sioux, you have to dance with me." She did beautiful snaky, spooky, arm dancing. Oh, the glamour!

I asked Siouxsie what her favorite book was. She replied, "*The Story of O*." That threw me. I had been avoiding that rather trendy book for years because I'd been at the mercy of men for so long I thought the last thing I'd want to read is a book about some chateau with women chained to the walls. Thinking of her, I was able to read the book by reversing the gender roles in my mind, and was even able to enjoy it. The book is about a secret club of rich men who turn fabulous '50s French fashion models into love slaves. The women all got paid a lot of money, which I found appealing since that wasn't usually the case in my experience. Reading the book I learned something about S&M, something about myself, and something about the world. This would not have been possible without the image of Siouxsie as a strong leather woman. The Marquis de Sade said the most important thing is to free yourself from inner prisons. Through meeting Siouxsie, I was inspired to keep working at it.

My friend Ginger's zine, *Punk Globe*, was a brilliantly bizarre mixture of gossip about the local punk scene and Ginger's other true passion, soap operas. She would call up people for quotes, not only her favorite rock stars, but movie and TV personalities. The zine would have articles about people like Joan Rivers and Ed Asner right next to articles about bands like Social Distortion and the Mutants.

When it reached its height of popularity, Punk Globe was being carried by Tower Records, Fiorucci, trendy stores in London, and had a circulation of five thousand. She often put my picture in it, and I often bought advertising space for my gigs at the Mabuhay. Ginger was friends with Joe Jackson, and when he played L.A. he paid for a suite at the Tropicana for her. She, I, and her photographer Julie went down to L.A. for a week.

The Tropicana was a Flintstones-looking motor lodge that was the place to stay for traveling music groups. The lobby was covered in 8x10 glossies of many famous guests: the Village People, Amanda Lear, and punk bands too numerous to mention. It was run by old queens, and also hosted numerous sexual rendezvous and unsavory underworld activities. The obnoxious closet queen Gene October and his band Chelsea (a spin-off of Billy Idol's original band Generation X) was staying there at the same time we were. He was always trying to be oh-so-punk, throwing chairs on stage and insulting Americans. We hung out with the band a lot, and Ginger scored big points when they found her listening to homemade audio tapes of *All My Children* by the pool. Those soap opera vixens were beyond punk. Tapes with dialogue like:

"I hope he DIES on that operating table!"

"Daisy Cortland, how could you wish death on someone? What has Palmer ever done to you?"

"Nothing, but I don't care!"

The headlines that week were all about Playboy centerfold Dorothy Stratton, who had been shot in the face by her jealous husband, an event later turned into the film *Star 80*. You could hear the cracking of whips through the walls of our room as the Mafia-produced S&M magazines were filmed across the courtyard. Duke's, the restaurant right downstairs, was a perfect place to see and be scene by the stars who were constantly arriving and or departing: people like Exene Cervenka, Stiv Bators and The Dead Boys, or The Cramps. This atmosphere was a surreal contrast to hanging out backstage at the Universal Amphitheater (where Joe Jackson was playing) with no less than Olivia Newton John, looking every inch a goddess in her blue satin warm-up jacket and skintight Fiorucci jeans.

I love L.A. because it looks like Bedrock. I adore that Hollywood energy. Also, you're never a hero in your hometown because people see you doing your laundry. I always have a great time in L.A. People give me things. As well they should. I'm a native Californian, I'm blond, I talk breathy, I have a total right to be accepted in L.A. Over the years, my love affair with the city of fallen angels has grown. On my almost yearly pilgrimages I've thoroughly enjoyed landmarks like Bullock's Wilshire Tea Room (full of starlets in their twilight years, wearing big hats), Spago, and the Coral Sands Hotel for porn stars.

Bambi, Brian & Danielle

Our Lady of the Wayside

One day, without warning, my decadent lifestyle began to go down the drain. Gloria got enormous breast implants. Gloria's wife, who had been living in Marin unaware of her spouse's extravagant transvestite fantasy life, couldn't miss them. This gave her fabulous grounds for divorce. I lost the credit cards, hair appointments, hormone treatments, everything. To make matters worse, my status at the Galaxy went from prima donna to doormat since Herbie blamed me when Gloria stopped paying on her enormous tab at the bar. Giving up my total maniacal/spoiled brat/drug addict/cocaine/fancy restaurant/Dilaudid prescription lifestyle was hell. To make matters worse, this happened just when Baba and Freddy had flown the nest, and then I turned thirty! I went on crying jags. I couldn't eat. I couldn't sleep. I wigged out.

Fortunately, Gloria still had enough money to send me to a psychiatrist. While discussing my love life, he pointed out, "These boys you're obsessing over are ten years younger than you." He kindly and clearly showed me that age difference was an important reason that the relationships ended. He suggested that I had to let go of my youth and think about my future. He told me that I could go out and become a model or an actress, and suggested the reason I hadn't was because I had an inferiority complex.

"No, I've got a superiority complex!" I shrieked.

"It amounts to the same thing," he replied.

That remark really hit home, and this is something a lot of queens deal with. The superiority complex results in the bitchiness queens are renowned for. It's a defense mechanism. The inferiority complex leads to the staggeringly high rate of suicide among transgendered people. Queens have to learn to overcome the heartbreak that comes from seeing yourself through the eyes of a world that does not respect or desire you. Depression can be the result of hating yourself, feeling inadequate. I had been looking at myself through the eyes of two twenty-year-old straight boys and coming up short. I learned to stop. This is all ABC psychiatry, but when it clicks, it can make a huge difference. After I saw that doctor, I never again had any suicidal tendencies or lasting depressions.

Alone and broke, I realized I was going to have to start over, professionally and personally. I'd spent a lot of time in North Beach hanging around straight punk rockers and strip joints. It was time to get back to my gay roots. I've always bounced back and forth between gay and straight clubs because I have two different agendas in my body. So like fallen royalty, I returned to Polk Street a marauder. Stranded, selling my jewels and pretty ball gowns, consorting with the local thieves and whores and pirates. I did a porn movie and used the money to get an apartment on Post Street.

Doing a porn film wasn't anything new to me. I had started doing porn films in the late '70s. Back then, they were very prejudiced against transsexuals. On this particular film, the German director really wanted me to fuck a girl, but I just can't have sex with women. I just can't do it. They kept bringing me this girl and that girl, and finally I did the scene with one of the girls I was working with at the Galaxy. This was very early in the she-male era, before Sulka. I was paid around six hundred dollars, enough for that studio apartment on Post Street.

The biggest porn film I appeared in was *The Return of Misty Beethoven* with Jamie Gillis and Constance Money. That was back when porn was a big deal, before AIDS. It was really an underworld scene, financed by Mafia money, and lots of the girls were strung out on coke. The local industry all got busted when a girl who was underage turned them in, and then disappeared into the Midwest. I had worked with the girl at the Galaxy, and the film producers wanted me to testify that she lied about her age and that she worked in a strip club, but I really didn't want to get involved with that. I mean, what kind of credibility did I have?

Anyway, I had earned enough money for an apartment. Things were looking grim but I still had my looks, new tits, and a newly trained singing voice.

I had returned to America to become a singer and now was the time. I went to piano bars like the Mint, the P.S., the Mask, and the Galleon, and sang Sondheim and old Gertrude Lawrence songs with all the sweater queens. They didn't know what to make of me at first but in time they accepted me and requested certain songs. It helped that my younger brother Kevin, who happened to be gay, was working at the P.S. We all drank a lot. My solo debut was at the Roxy Roadhouse. No reviewers, just guys from the Polk Street piano bars came. I played there every other Tuesday for six months, selling tickets out of my purse. I bought vintage gowns, met the better pianists, and schmoozed hairdressers.

Around that time punk died, and I was sick of it anyway. But I did like to hang out around the hardcore scene that was taking its place, mostly for the pure titillation of viewing the Roman Coliseum atmosphere provided by the young sweaty male slam pit/ skateboard circus. I had always been considered something of a novelty act, but once testosterone-drenched bands became the norm, I stood out all the more. Once I sang a Bowie song, "Lady Stardust," at a show with The Mutants and L.A.'s Black Flag. Well, Black Flag came back to town for another gig right after Henry Rollins, the lead singer, had just given some interview saying he was into Nastassja Kinski because she was so tough. That week she'd posed in *Playboy* for Helmut Newton as Dietrich, so I went backstage at their show, and said, "Would you like me to sing my Dietrich songs in my see-through black lace dress which is a copy of what Nastassja Kinski wore in *Playboy*?" He said okay, and the girls at the show just couldn't believe I'd been backstage with the ever-attractive Henry Rollins. So I performed my Dietrich set in front of an audience composed of very butch hardcore kids and skinheads.

The tape that accompanied me for my Dietrich songs was recorded by an old woman. It was as if she had taken a handful of valium, and the tempo was exceedingly slow. It made the audience very angry at first, but I used my boudoir powers to get through to the guys. The power of the black and pink lace garter. It's a groupie thing. Sweet Pam from the Cockettes lived with Dee Dee Ramone for years because she had the hottest lingerie in New York. You use that on those boys because they will fall. Always use fishnets, always use heels. It continues to work and will always work.

Since losing my job at the Galaxy, I was working out of the Road Runner, a legendary TS hooker bar on O'Farrell and Jones. Once, as I was leaving the bar, a souped-up, bad-ass roadrunner mobile drove up and a man inside asked me to get in. Until that time, I thought all undercover police cars were dorky looking. That one wasn't. They took me to a precinct police station off Polk Street where there was a holding cell containing a drunken derelict getting beaten by the cops. They threw me in and said, "Give him some head." Needless to say, I declined. I was then transferred to the downtown station where I was held with more drunks who called me a fag and acted really scary. I felt particularly vulnerable with my big tits, but was somewhat heartened that I was wearing an attractive new leather bomber jacket from Wilsons. I spent the next day in the queens' tank listening to screaming madmen in solitary across the hall, using the frightening public toilets, and eating horrible, wretched food. They even lined us up, chained us all together with handcuffs, and then made us march! The D.A. told me to plead guilty if I wanted to get out that day, so I did. This time I didn't get fined, but was forced to attend Monday night meetings at the Center for Special Problems.

The Center for Special Problems was very *One Flew Over the Cuckoo's Nest*. It was run by two big Nurse Ratched types and there were bars on the windows. They made all the queens sit in a circle and tell horror stories about their wasted lives. There were all the usual tales of marginalized individuals: inability to get a job, alcoholism, drug abuse, *blah blah blah*. The nurses showed marked favoritism towards the prettier queens, who would get SSI and typing lessons. I would sass the staff mercilessly, pointing out that they weren't about to help the rest of us get jobs but instead expected us to sit around and whine for no apparent reason. My last Monday meeting came right after I'd spent all day in Tiburon making a porn film with Shauna Grant and John Leslie.

Around that time, I went to see an English band, The Stranglers, when they played the Stone. That night I went back to their hotel, for a very memorable encounter with the bass player. I called *Melody Maker* in London after it happened and told them the story, and they actually printed it. Later the Stranglers came to see my show at the Roxy Roadhouse and brought Robin Williams with them! They

arranged for me to open for them the next night doing my Dietrich
stuff at the enormous Kabuki Theater.

Chiclet, Bambi & Connie

Hello?... Excuse Me?... La Dolce Vita

I was so well received at the Kabuki that the Stranglers invited me on their "In Search of Paradise Midnight Summer Dream" European tour. Thirty stadiums in France, Italy, and Spain in thirty days, darling! I went from being Polk Street trash to living a jet set, Monte Carlo fantasy life... Speeding along freeways in their red Mercedes making sex noises with the bass player in the back seat... The day I arrived in Paris, I was filmed for a TV commercial for the tour. In the commercial I was having simulated sex in a fabulous warehouse with a pretty French boy wearing a Stranglers t-shirt and playing pinball. Traveling up the coast of Spain in a tour bus we passed '50s *La Dolce Vita*-style resort areas where Amanda Lear carried on her affair with Bryan Ferry.

I worked hard on that tour. Some nights the audience would

throw things at me, and I had to work really hard to earn their respect. As the tour progressed, I learned more and more about how to win the audience over, and by the end they were giving me encores. At the time, the Stranglers' European audience, unlike San Francisco, was a mainstream rock crowd, and they found my Dietrich act very challenging.

Living and working so closely with the members of the band while on tour was great for the most part, but it wasn't easy. One time I cut myself shaving, and had a teeny, tiny piece of toilet paper stuck to my neck to stop the bleeding, and the band teased me mercilessly, "You have to shave?!?"

Another time, while in France, the bass player got furious because I cut the paté wrong. Can you imagine? All the meals were catered, and sometimes the food was better than others.

Next comes, without a doubt, THE STUPIDEST THING I EVER DID. After the tour ended, without calling first, I hopped on a train to Berlin. I had no desire to return to America. In 1983, there was no place in any quadrant of society for transsexuals. Punk had given way to hardcore which was all about machismo, and there were scary skinheads everywhere. I had no real interest in that scene beyond occasionally teasing the boys. One party consisted of all these skinheads eating acid-laced Cheerios. My friend and I had fun trying to sell them all the Tupperware from the kitchen, but by and large, I had no interest in them. By returning to Berlin, I had hoped to lead a fabulous, sexy, and exciting life once again.

As in every fairytale, there were some scary moments. Romy Haag was gone. The club's new owner let me stay with him but I couldn't handle the slick new choreography he had introduced into the show. Sugar was working at Chez Nous but they weren't hiring. It was winter. One miserable night, I lost my key and spent the night freezing like the little match girl on the stoop. I finally got a job at the Laughbunner, doing "Le Jazz Hot," the song from *Victor Victoria*.

Then, in a bizarre delayed reaction to my night in the snow on the stoop, my face froze. The doctors were mystified. Their brilliant diagnosis was Facialis Paralysis, which they said was evidently very common after WWII. "Ve hafseen zis very much, it comes from not eating good." They were of no help. Being unable to smile, I lost my job.

Things looked bleak when along came a good Samaritan (and closet crossdresser with an amazing wardrobe), Franz, who took me to Nuremberg where I lived as his hausfrau for a few months. He used to take me on weekend excursions. We saw Rothenburg, the touristy thirteenth-century walled city, and Neuschwanstein, the winter castle of Mad King Ludwig, on which the Disney *Sleeping Beauty* castle is based. Our most incredible destination was Garmisch, the swanky ski village on the Austrian border, replete with hoity-toity tea shops with big chunky crystal chandeliers everywhere, swirling snowstorms swathing everything in sight, and furs, furs, furs. It was an opulent fantasy. One half-expected Liz Taylor to walk in at any moment.

At home, life with Franz was surreal. We were on a strict clockwork schedule every day, which began when he would lay out a sumptuous pastry breakfast and ask, "Is it good enough for mice? I think it's just good enough for mice." You see, he was obsessed with Beatrix Potter's mice stories. Everything I had was mice: I had mice shoes, a mice coat. It just didn't stop. Franz eventually convinced the American Embassy to send me home. Unfortunately, his phone number was lost, and I've never been able to thank him properly.

Back in San Francisco, I went to General Hospital for my Facialis Paralysis and was told I had Bell's Palsy, which they said was incurable. Some Chinese guys I met in a restaurant told me to try acupuncture. It worked. I was cured in a week. Sometimes the ignorance of western medicine is amazing. I delved back into stripping at the Galaxy and singing. The old North Beach punk scene was being replaced by the '80s fashion club-hopper cocktails thing in SOMA, the Mission, and the Castro. I moved with the times.

I did a Vargas Pin-up Girl/Film Noir/Hollywood/1940s theme act, performing at Club 181, Club 9, and DV8. "Moon Over Miami," "I Wish I Knew," "Do Right," "Marne," "You Do," "I Can't Begin to Tell You." I also had my Occupied Paris nightclub act called "Cafe Megalomania," with these intense college boys who sat around reading Nietzsche all day. They would try and get me to pretend to be on heroin and act like a Nazi ice goddess. I had to stop because it was all getting too real, too much like the Weimar Republic. This was the ultraconservative mid-'80s. Gays stopped going out during the first years of the AIDS crisis, and all the gay clubs turned into yuppie hangouts. Straight people didn't want to hang around with gays or queens anymore either.

1984 was in many ways just as ugly as Orwell had predicted. I was drinking heavily and having confrontations in trendy nightclubs with people who couldn't deal with transsexuals, much less talented transsexuals with attitudes. I quit Cafe Megalomania, and put together my Betty Grable act as a reaction against that whole creepy, right wing, trendy, Teutonic chic. In protest I wanted to become an All American Fag Heroine. Nobody understood.

Drag performance is infused with camp sensibility that deconstructs and satirizes the culture of previous generations. In the '70s, queens would do '30s and '40s camp. By the '80s, it was the '50s and '60s. Betty Grable had given way to Bewitched. To appeal to a new generation, I started becoming more fluid with my material. I will always love the Cockettes sensibility but for a while I had to put it in a little velvet box and forget about it, let it appreciate in value.

Around that time, Gere Finelly invited me to open for her band, Pennsylvania Mahoney, which also featured Gail from Tragic Mulatto and members of Polkacide, at their weekly Tuesday night gigs at the Paradise Lounge. Gere accompanied me on her portable baby grand piano that she'd painted pink. Gere is a biological girl who's played piano in a myriad of bands ranging in genre from heavy metal to gothic to cocktail music. She was most recently playing with Redd Kross. She's cute and smiley and fun. A lot of the old punk crowd from the Mabuhay ended up down at the Paradise. It was Punk Cabaret, a trend with which I was completely copacetic. Slowly, with weekly gigs, good sound, and a receptive audience, the singing voice I had waited for finally emerged out of my throat. People stopped and listened, and applauded... really loud. My repertoire included "Blue Velvet," "Hey Daddy," "Cry Me A River," "Black Coffee," "Where The Boys Are," and "Wild Is The Wind." We also took the act to other nightclubs around town, including DNA, 13%, and Das Klub.

Throughout this time I was trying to quit speed permanently and become self-sufficient. My name was appearing often in the club calendar listings. I schmoozed more hairdressers. Visits to Dorothy Starr's sheet music outlet expanded my repertoire of songs. The gay punk boys became my first real fans. They understood all of my references and innuendoes. They appreciated rock and drag and cabaret and show tunes. Starting with them, I began developing my own audience and getting a bit of fame. You can't coattail it, you need your own hit single, and you have to start at the bottom. Unfortunately, even the bottom wasn't very accessible. In the first rush of AIDSphobia, queer entertainers became box office poison. Not only was it harder than ever to get a good gig opening for a popular band, it was even hard to get backstage to meet people. There were, of course, a few exceptions like Nina Hagen. I went backstage to meet her once, and when I mentioned Romy and Sugar whom she knew from Berlin, her apocalyptic sci-fi facade dropped, and we got along famously. She said Bambi was the nickname of her baby daughter, Cosmo Shiva.

I found another audience in the '80s with death rockers.

Somehow glamorous junkies have always gravitated in my direction, and the goth set thought it was the funniest thing to have me sing backed by 101 Strings. And they just adored my German act. I opened for Specimen and the Jesus and Mary Chain at the Anti-Easter, doing a sort of TS Elvira look. The Butthole Surfers, who weren't famous yet, opened for me!

Around this time as well, I became Frightwig's official opening act. Frightwig is the ultimate all-girl punk band: they were riot grrrls before there was such a thing. The band started in '82, are still around, and are revered for their longevity, musical virtuosity, and wit. They invited me to open for them and Mary Housecoat in L.A. The show was so packed that Mike Ness of Social Distortion couldn't even get in, and the *L.A. Weekly* referred to me as San Francisco's most famous transsexual. Frightwig stayed in their van parked at the beach, and they brought a bunch of cute little boys out there to party with them. In the airport they had a running joke about trying to scam money out of the automatic teller machine, saying "Work it, girl, work it hard, work it like a Visa card." That line was eventually worked into the chorus of a song called "Beverly." The cheap midnight flights to and from S.F. were always hysterically funny.

Since getting back from the Stranglers tour, I had been living on and off with Electra, a soundman who had worked with the Cockettes and at the Mabuhay Gardens. He's a long haired, androgynous, easygoing electrical genius. He is renown throughout San Francisco, and soon became my guardian angel. He made sure I had somewhere to stay, ate properly, and got me gigs. As a technical sound wizard, he made sure I sounded right, got enough "headroom," the right amount of reverb, and the best mikes. You can't imagine how important that can be when playing in clubs with mediocre to lousy sound systems.

When the Stranglers came to San Francisco in '87, they gave me free passes, but my old flame, the bass player, refused to talk to me at soundcheck. Even worse, I was humiliated in front of my friends when they wouldn't let me visit backstage. What churls! Recently I called the bass player, and he said, "Well, fuck me sideways! Where are you calling from?" When I mentioned his snub, he apologized, saying, "Sorry, Luv, I musta been on smack. I'd never treat you like that... we were mates. God bless you."

1987 was also the year disaster struck. The Galaxy closed for good and things got rather ugly. I had no job skills and I was heading back to welfare, a situation I hadn't seen for fifteen years. I became an unwilling regular at the notorious Black Rose on Jones and Eddy Streets in the Tenderloin. It was a large cocktail lounge with a very long bar which was specifically patronized by transsexual hookers and their johns. I made survival money by hooking there. I dressed in a 1980s supermodel style: very high black pumps, black tights or fishnets, black stretch mini-dress with various bitchy little suit jackets, my favorite being a faux-English riding jacket. I was very underweight: one hundred twenty pounds (which when you're six feet tall can look great but is rather unhealthy). I'd go there in the morning, bum a cigarette and coffee, then try and get a trick to buy me something to eat.

A lot of my friends thought the place was fabulous with its over the top, cyber-sex, Frankenhooker atmosphere. They didn't have to work there. The atmosphere was funny, grotesque, and erotically supercharged all at once. Beautiful transsexuals and the scariest transsexuals you ever met all lumped into one zone. The worst part was when the bar would close, and you hadn't made a date. You had to wander up to Post and Larkin and stand around in the cold for hours while the cars with johns circled around. Sometimes you'd have to wait for hours to make your forty bucks. The queens were nasty, and the tricks expected you to pass. This life was not for me and I shudder to think I lived that way. I couldn't believe I was trapped there. What miracle would save me?

One day some queen was buying me shots at the Polk Gulch Saloon and I got plastered. Outside I got in a car and propositioned a vice cop who recognized me from Broadway. "You're the one with the legs!" He let me off with a ticket. At the hearing, I wore flawless Chanel knock-offs and was amused to see the court secretaries working the same look. The third offense could have meant time in the county jail, but my arrests were spread out over ten years so they referred me to A.A. instead, which probably helped me. I ended up going to meetings at the First Place, which had a small transsexual contingent. For the first time I realized that transsexuality didn't have to be synonymous with low self-esteem and methedrine addiction. I'm not currently in a program, but it certainly helped that I spent time in one.

Frustrated artistically — I was a novelty act opening for other people — and needing work, I took my press clippings, great reviews of my shows from the weekly gay papers, and marched into Finocchio's, the famous drag joint for tourists that's been operating on Broadway for over fifty years. They don't like to hire transsexuals but I convinced them to reconsider, promising not to show too much cleavage. Finocchio's epitomizes the school of female impersonation that is "All In Fun." It's like a minstrel show, keep them laughing. The audience consists of loud, drunk, suburban, conservative tourists. You don't dare get too close to the audience, and you certainly don't kiss bald men's heads or sit on laps like you could before AIDS paranoia set in.

I did my best but it was just not my type of place, although there were good points. First of all, I went from making twenty dollars every other week at the Paradise to earning the princely sum of three hundred and fifty bucks a week while working only four hours a night. They still had a live band back then as well as a lovely backstage: old, spacious, and comfortable. One highlight was working with legendary Laura de los Santos, the reigning queen there. Laura sometimes took hormones but when she did the club would threaten to fire her. Fortunately she was so exquisitely beautiful she didn't really need them. The management was so uptight they even made her cover her beautiful long black hair with a wig and harassed her for leaving work in drag. I loved listening to her stories about having sex with Tony Danza in Beverly Hills, told in her thick, clipped, Filipino accent. She was the terror of Polk Street, picking up hustlers in her sporty Mustang. It was a rare gesture of transsexual sisterhood when she let me onto her turf.

To succeed at Finocchio's, you had to be either totally gorgeous or totally funny. My style is very different. I share things I think are amusing, but my own femininity is not a joke. I try to look nice, but I am not a female illusionist or a beauty queen. Trying to reveal and express myself, and communicate new ideas through transgender performance is my focus, while fighting the old tired rude trip Finocchio's has pushed all these years. What finally compelled me to get out wasn't the tiredness though, but the mice that infested the place. The other performers were, underneath all the glamour, men. They didn't care. I would stand on my chair shrieking when I saw the little rodent monsters. I thought I saw my old childhood pal David's mom in the audience once, but I never found out for sure.

Boner Babes

Luckily, another way to make a living soon presented itself. I met Emily, a.k.a. Ernesto, a little Latin queen with a shady past, at the Black Rose. She was doing phone sex work as a woman, and running an ad in *The Spectator*, an adult swinger magazine featuring picture ads of she-male call girls. Soon I was living with her, running my own ad, and having gentlemen callers. It was great to do sex work and not to have to hide who I was, like at the Galaxy, where I had to tuck and lie about being a woman.

Working as a she-male call girl was sort of fun and sort of weird. Straight men in and out, and long hours at home, waiting in my boudoir decorated like a Belle Époque Parisian courtesan with feathers, corsets, and a vanity table laden with pearls and perfume and jewels. I'd finally decided to have silicone added to my lips, face, and hips. I looked good but still not like the kind of TS men like to take out: I'm not that perfectly passable. Despite electrolysis, my facial hair can still be a problem. Also, I'm unusually tall. But men did love private sessions with me. These men, many of them gorgeous buffed young military types, wanted me to fuck them. They wanted to give me head. These guys were so sure of themselves they could trade roles with me. They all said they weren't attracted to other men and I think a lot of them did date women. I offered them something else. She-male porn films started it all, Sulka and Kim Christy films: they gave men a taste for she-male sex. It's something between a cult and a fetish.

I had a couple of beautiful Latin yuppie guys who saw me on a regular basis, always to get fucked. My most fascinating caller was a Latin bodybuilder army hero. He took my picture with him to the Persian Gulf, and returned wounded from Somalia, for which he's getting a Purple Heart. He told me he chose me to be the first queen to fuck him. His crotch smelled incredible and I hated having to use a condom to suck him off. He looked like a Brazilian soap opera star: dark eyed, square jawed, pouty lipped, smoldering. The first time he came over, he stripped and laid himself out, and said "Do you like what you see?" I was trying to control my lust, and act nonchalant, but I was humbled by the sight of him. He toyed with me. He even kissed. He was better than my movie idol, Matt Dillon. He was a war hero, and he paid me.

Hector, a straight, young, cute, Hispanic dude answered my ad. I gave him head, only charged him forty bucks, and said he could be my boyfriend. He didn't call again till a year later. When he did, he said he wanted to suck my dick. I said he'd still have to pay 'cause he didn't call back for a year, and invited him over. He said it was too late, he had to get up early. So I decided to get him off over the phone. I said, "I've got a really big dick and I want you to lift my skirt, pull down my panties and suck me off. Stick out your butt, you bad boy, I'm going to pin you down, spread your legs, and fuck your pretty butthole." I told him to stick his finger in his ass and suck the come out of my dick. He got really hot. I said, "Suck my big dick, you hot little bitch." He came all over his chest. The next day we played it out for real.

I am a very sexual person. I've never had the money for sex change surgery, just hormones and implants and such, so I've learned to enjoy my situation as a she-male. It's very important to know what you want and find your type. I'm not a swinger at all. I hate group sex. I've either had sex for money (though never with really ugly people) or with very gorgeous men. Yet it's always been exceedingly private, though I do love to brag about it later. I'm not interested in the submission of the lovely feminine she-male, but the overdue fulfillment of queens with grade A quality male flesh. It's very multicultural; I like all races. Anyway, the point is that my life isn't camp or tragic, it's gorgeous and sexy and nothing like *The Crying Game* or *M Butterfly*. When I have sex with straight men it's because they want a she-male, and when it's good, it's totally new, important and legendary.

There are times when I wonder what my life would be like if I could pass well enough to work at a nice boutique, or what it would be like to be the head of a male modeling agency. I have an extremely acute appreciation of male beauty. Dealing with beautiful guys is sort of like being a lion tamer. I'd love to have a whip, a whistle, wear really great thigh boots, and have muscle boys leaping through hoops for me.

What would my life be like as a well-connected celebrity hairdresser in New York? I'd really live life. The hairdressers of New York are bi-coastal, they're flown out to work with their clients at the Academy Awards, they're just drinking, eating beef jerky, making the rudest remarks, and they're right in on life. They know everything about everyone. They know the truth about Michael Jackson and the boys, O.J. Simpson, the movie star and the gerbils.

Where was I? Oh, as I was saying, Emily (the queen with a shady past who turned me onto *The Spectator*) was renting a storefront on Divisadero Street and fixing it up as a hat store. She often stayed there and left me to work at the apartment, which she had painted entirely black, floor and all. We went to the Salvation Army and bought a champagne velvet living room set. I added to this madness by decorating with dollhouse touches, French Victorian lady prints, Dresden statues, and Persian rugs. We opened a club at the hat store on Saturdays called the Hat Box Club that featured poetry and cabaret. It was quite a chic little hot spot for a while, and drinks were served by our live-in butler. I also met Emily's girlfriend, Danielle Willis, who was working as a stripper at the Mitchell Brothers' O'Farrell Theater.

Danielle was about twenty-one years old, worked a tweaky goth/ dominatrix/rock star look and had published a book of ingenious, dark baroque, Tenderloin, dyke, fantasy poetry and stories. We took to each other immediately. She was from a very privileged background and had a total fascination with transsexual hookers. I was starting to get sort of empowered by the new queer/dyke/sexworker/fuck you movement, of which Danielle was a major instigator. I would tell her endless stories about my long history as a queen in the now fashionable '70s, and she delighted in my casual literary references. She helped me overcome my Catholic guilt about sex work, but to this day, I still don't want my mother to know.

Danielle cast me in her play, *The Methedrine Dollhouse*, a dark comedy that was performed at the Exit Theater in the Tenderloin. The play was about a female and she-male dominatrix duo living with an ex-Nazi movie star/slasher film producer in Beverly Hills. It's a great play, funny and scary at the same time. Danielle wrote it at a summer writers' colony that Kate Millet runs on her farm. She used to send me little care packages from the farm with money, *My*

Comrade magazines, and 3-D Jayne Mansfield comic books. The play was a hit, and I was pleased that I still had the brainpower to memorize a lead role.

My character was supposed to snort some speed on stage, which made me uncomfortable. I had not quite shaken the monkey off my back, and it was hard for me to play that for laughs. I had always been privy to the highest grade biker speed because of my old connections, and that made it even harder to kick. The way methedrine affects me is reminiscent of *A Midsummer Night's Dream*. Now step aside, chirren, an' let Mama quote the Bard. You will recall that Oberon and Titania were fighting over a changeling boy when Oberon told Puck to fetch an enchanted aphrodisiac flower. "Fetch me that herb and with it I'll streak her eyes and make her full of hateful fantasies," and, "The juice of this herb when squeezed upon sleeping eyes will make one madly dote upon the first thing that one waking sees." It's just like that with me and methedrine, I fall for anything as long as it's male.

As the '80s ended, San Francisco was starting to happen again. The conformist, yuppie, Reagan reality was giving way to renewed activism and cultural vitality. Performing at a SmutFest, one of Jennifer Blowdryer's hugely popular sexworker-oriented spoken word/performance evenings, was as fun as working with The Popstitutes, a manic queer musical performance art troupe. Choreographing a stage full of twisted kids in a lewd Bob Fosse-like dance for a nightclub show was great. Diet and Alvin, friends since my Polk Street punk days, started Klubstitute, a queer cabaret. It attracted a real mix of types, and when I started singing there, a whole new audience was instantly hip to my style of performance. I did everything from Jane's Addiction to Velvet Underground songs, and they loved it.

As an eternal punk rock girl, it's very important to enjoy the artistic freedom to play around with my act and incorporate all sorts of influences. I don't want to be stuck just singing old show tunes. When I do a diva, be it Marlene Dietrich or Rickie Lee Jones, reinterpreting and embodying an archetype in a very individual way is essential. I never try to be someone else. Also, the same old divas can be remarkably tiresome. I've been through Greta Garbo, Marilyn Monroe, Lotte Lenya, Judy Garland, Rita Hayworth, Betty Grable, Peggy Lee, and Julie London. Recently it was Ann-Margret: the female Elvis, the oomph girl, the showstopper. Doing her takes guts and confidence. While I may not possess her glowing smile, doing her gives me the chance to express my sexy side. Her ballads are really the ultimate sex kitten ballads: "Bachelor in Paradise," "I Want To Be Loved," and her up-tempo "The Swinger" rocks! She represents the new drag (groovy rather than grande dame) because she wore bellbottoms. I do my tribute to her in transparent beaded ones.

Of course, divas aren't my sole performance focus anymore. As a singer/songwriter, my work is very consciously modeled on Joni Mitchell, one of my biggest influences. I've been a fan of hers since the '60s. I love the simplicity of hearing just a woman and her guitar: it's classic, perennial. When I went on tour with the Angels of Light, they used to kid around and call me Joni (I do look a bit like her) and beg me to sing, which I would. It became a running bit and after a while I could mimic her flawlessly. At the Vorpal Gallery in 1980 when I actually got to meet her, I couldn't resist the temptation to imitate her to her face, brazenly blurting out the first verse of "For The Roses." She laughed. We ended up leaving the gallery at the same time, and as I waited for my taxi and she for her limo, she stared at me. I think there's really something special about meeting people like Siouxsie or Bowie or Joni. They're so advanced and alien. It's like they've come from outer space and there's a B-movie mental telepathy energy transfer from them to you.

Around this time I made another foray into pop music fronting a death rock industrial group called Exterminating Angel. We were sort of like proto-Laibach or pre-Nine Inch Nails, early industrial dance music. Our image was cyberpunk prostitute assassins on Mars. I wore metal breast cones (before Madonna, thank you very much) and lots of black vinyl and leather. In the end, it was too tough for me, coming up with dance music commercial enough for college radio. You have to have magic qualities of total genius for that. I was in Exterminating Angel for six months in 1989, and six major trends were happening at any given moment in modern rock at the time... you were passé the next day. The equipment and computers necessary for that kind of music were also extraordinarily expensive. Confronting a straight rock audience was still a trip. They'd say things like, "I remember you from the 181 Club and you, like, wanted to suck my dick, and for a dude, you're really like a chick, man." I'd rather just run back to a piano bar and start singing Sondheim. I just couldn't do that again, make myself the target.

I eventually split from Emily and ended up with another mad queen, Victoria, who'd created the lighting for *The Methedrine Dollhouse*. She'd also designed the lights for the Mona Rogers show, worked with George Coates, and the latter-day Angels of Light. I worked my ad with her in Bernal Heights. Victoria's apartment was right over a three-star Italian restaurant and was an ideal place for attracting dates. Soon I was making real money. I bought a new fancy wardrobe at MAC and lots of new hippie velvety things at Na Na. Then I took a vacation in Hollywood where I stayed at the Coral Sands and went to all the clubs: the Queen Mary, Atlas, Sit and Spin, the Mayan, and my favorite, Peanuts, a long-running club in Los Angeles for TS hookers. It's clean and fun, full of exquisite bitch goddess Hollywood transsexuals. The night I went I wore a black vinyl mini-dress and a leather trench coat, and left with the drummer from the punk band, The Misfits. Of course I also went to Frederick's of Hollywood and spent four hundred dollars on shoes. That trip to

Los Angeles was a rite of passage. I was seen by transsexual society and had a blast.

Back in San Francisco, Phillip R. Ford, director of the cult classic movie *Vegas in Space* and countless local drag events, was impressed by my act at the Albion. Through him, I met and befriended the Sluts a Go Go: Tippi, Miss X, and Doris Fish. Our paths had crossed for years but we'd never really connected. Doris was in The Tubes show back in the '70s when my friend Kenny had choreographed them, and we'd seen each other at parties where Doris was invariably dressed as a maid. All through the '80s, she and the other Sluts were all over the club scene in their day-glo pop '60s finery. The whole TS hooker world was starting to feel creepy, and it was nice to be able to hang around smart, friendly, successful show business people. Holidays had always been strange and depressing since I was never invited home; around this time I started spending Christmas with Phil and the Sluts (who really do it up big time) which made me have more of *A Wonderful Life.*

Doris became ill, and a benefit held for her at the Victoria Theater was called *Who Does That Bitch Think She Is?* I sang "Waltzing Matilda" since Doris was Australian, and the song drew a standing ovation from the sold-out theater. It was a very emotional moment, up there in front of the whole town, singing for the dying diva. Marc Huestis, a local filmmaker and powerhouse promoter, was moved enough to produce a solo show for me at a popular club in the Castro, Josie's Cabaret & Juice Joint, which was a real breakthrough. I called my parents to give them the good news. My dad started in with his old line, "Oh, John, I remember you in *The Music Man.* You were so great." I had to tell him, "Dad, John is dead. I've been Bambi for almost twenty years. This is not a passing phase." I think he finally got it.

The show was called, *BAMBI! An Evening of Song and Revelation.* I talked about my life from A to Z: Cockettes, Berlin, punk, South of

Market. Thanks to the recognition achieved by working with well-known producers like Phil and Marc, everyone in town turned out for the show. My brother Kevin was also very helpful when it came to getting people in to see the show, talking it up in Castro bars. He also got my family, who I think were very curious, to come and see it. The guilt-ridden nightmares about my mother, where we engage in shouting matches, stopped when she came to see the show. I acknowledge part of my survival has been because my mother was a saint. She didn't go around wearing a housecoat and drinking beer out of a can. She worked hard to raise eight kids with a husband who wasn't always around. Thanks, Mom!

It was fascinating to try and explain transsexualism to gays and lesbians. Some nights all the boys would show up and hoot and holler over the stories about the Berlin pimps. Other nights the girls would show up and be entranced by stories of heartbreak and loneliness and triumph. Although people loved the show, things didn't always go smoothly. One night I was discussing the mysteries of she-male orgasm: on female hormones you often cum dry, which Romy Haag had said was more feminine, and I got hissed by a lesbian separatist. On the whole, the show was a hit, and twenty-year-olds were now calling me a legend.

The show had to sell out six nights in order to break even financially, which happened thanks to great reviews in the gay press. The straight press didn't mention the show though, so an extended run wasn't possible and I made no profit. Working on the show required so much time that I got a month behind on my rent. I'll always want to do all that: sing Cockettes songs, wear old gowns, do Dietrich, come down staircases singing French at the top of my lungs, but it'd be nice to earn enough to pay my rent.

Marc Huestis produced my show at Josie's Cabaret & Juice Joint around the same time he produced the documentary film, *Sex Is…* I was the token white tranny in the film, and was asked questions about what it's like to be a transsexual. The movie emphasized sexual experiences: the filmmakers were interested in my views of what sex is (of course), and what an orgasm feels like. I floundered. I quoted Jean Genet, something about a constantly withering rose, and the audience just groaned. But I did get some good one-liners in. They wanted to know what we do while having sex, and how it works, so I finally said, "Well, you know, they're reaching up for your tits while sucking your dick, and you turn them over and fuck 'em in the ass." The audience loved that line. So often they show disdain for the poetry of an experience but enjoy the sordid descriptions. The film ran at the marvelous Castro Theater, and it was a thrill to be seen on the big screen.

Shortly thereafter, Victoria and I parted ways when she moved another transsexual on whom she had a crush into the apartment. After much begging and borrowing, I got a place on Valencia where I continued to work my ad, although the money was nowhere near as good in the new downscale location. With all its inherent problems, sex work is, as Danielle Willis says, one of the best art grants going.

BORED ON THE FOURTH OF JULY

It's the Fourth of July
I haven't made any money
on my *Spectator* ad
I never do on holidays
the tricks stay home
with their families
When I stripped on Broadway
it was the same way
It's a slow profound boredom
I've listened to all my tapes
I can't watch TV anymore

145

I haven't seen the sun in weeks
I can hear the clock tick
Tired, Tired, Tireder
Jet lag, reruns
commercials, waiting rooms
I suppose I should be hard at work
on my career as a queen/star

Shortly after Josie's, I got a call from the Paradise Lounge asking me to host a sort of Drag/TS Night on a weekly basis. I met with the owner and proposed my vision, a club based on New York's Pyramid Club and Boy Bar, a weekly showcase featuring San Francisco, New York, and Los Angeles stars, and my own rock band doing a different show each week. I wanted fabulous three-color posters, and a wardrobe budget. Well, it all happened perfectly! Sophia Lamar was flown in to open the club. Sophia has really helped me deal with life on a lot of levels. She lived on Polk Street in the '80s and now hosts clubs in New York. One of her most admirable qualities is her total lack of need for men. She goes out with her gay boy companions and pursues fame, has sex when she needs to, and that's it. She used to depress me because it's impossible to compete with her cool charm, yet I was delighted to be flying her in to open my club, which I decided to call Forbidden Planet. A few weeks later, Warhol superstar Holly Woodlawn was flown in to perform, and was paid royally. My dream of being a Romy Haag type proprietress of a sizzling nightspot was finally coming true. The club was a transsexual first because, not only wasn't it a hooker bar, it wasn't a karaoke type format either. There was a live band. The singers were being taken seriously in a club that had an established reputation and paid actual money.

It's always fun for queens to hang out together in a relaxed environment. There's a whole history to drag and transsexual showbiz, and when you're with a group of real show queens you will always hear the names fly. Coccinelle, Bambi (the original), and Capucine of Paris. Tula, and Holly White of England. Holly Woodlawn, Jackie Curtis and Candy Darling, the Warhol superstars. The runway models, Teri Toye, Connie Girl, Girlena, Sophia. San Francisco's incomparable Sluts A Go Go. Each name evokes pretty images and stories. Now in the '90s there's a new wave of drag, the Wigstock stars: RuPaul (the consummate showbiz pop star icon), Lady Bunny, Lahoma. The new drag is more silly, tongue in cheek. While I always tend to be a little grand and melancholy, I do find the new drag appealing.

Drag, my dear, is an art: ever-changing, very amusing, always fun. An important influence on today's drag was the '60s French transsexuals who emphasized realness and sophistication rather than exaggeration or camp. It's a school of art, it's my territory, and following developments closely is important. My identity is really based in that ideal filtered through the glamorous sensibility of the Warhol superstars. Keeping in touch with the artistic side of being a TS has always been essential. It's sad to see a transsexual whose life is only about surviving in the Tenderloin, turning tricks, doing drugs, and trying not to get killed. It's important to get along in the world and show young little boys what's possible, if they want it. I'm always urging my fellow lovelies to pursue a career, to make something substantial of themselves. Not only street hookers but even smart hip transsexual scenesters fall into a trap of just posing.

Not that posing isn't really hard work. Electrolysis, cosmetic surgery, Retin A, silicone. But frankly, transsexuals who are only interested in passing and assimilation in society are bit boring. I'm still a drag queen as well as a transsexual. Psychologists try to make a big differentiation between transsexuality on one hand, and transvestitism, homosexuality, and drag on the other. They try to force transsexuals out of the gay scene before they allow them to get the final operation. It's typical for many transsexuals to shun the world of drag and lose their senses of humor when they make the change, not only because of the psychologists, but also because they want to be taken seriously as a woman and not be laughed at as camp.

I never bought into that. I started out doing drag for artistic reasons. It was theater, and I see no reason to abandon it because of my gender status. Drag (in this context) is just a campy, exaggerated, theatrical presentation. Biological girls do drag, too! I like to mix with all sorts of people, and transsexuals have the unique perspective to be ambassadors between the gay and straight worlds, as well as between the sexes.

People see transsexuals and drag queens on TV talking about their rights, but that's not the whole picture. We transsexuals have our own little world; we have to actually, since there's so much prejudice out there. When I went on hormones (in the parlance of the porn world, became a "she-male"), I joined the pre-op transsexual underground network. You meet others of your kind and learn how to survive. With some luck, and especially if you can pass, a real job might be available, but as previously mentioned, lots of she-males have to survive as strippers or call girls. When it comes to show business, well, the movies and mainstream theater just aren't ready yet. They let women play transsexuals but transsexuals can't play women. No matter how convincing you appear, forget trying to pass as a woman in show business. Everybody knows and everybody tells; it's impossible to keep being transsexual secret. Things are changing though. Now you can get modeling jobs as an out transsexual. It's called Special Assignment. Our time has come!

Ramona Rechy once said back in Berlin that getting the operation is the ultimate disguise: "You must have the perfect disguise. What are they looking for? A woman. And when you are that, they will go crazy. And then you will go crazy."

Unfortunately, I wasn't born a girl. If the doctors whose

permission I need to get a full sex change read these stories and think because I like topping men sexually that means I'm happy as a pre-op, they might deny me my surgery if I eventually try to do it. I'm willing to risk that. This is a wickedly difficult topic and my feelings about this fluctuate from day to day. If I'd had the money to get a full sex change I probably would have done it long ago. In the final analysis, I identify as female.

I've always enjoyed surrendering to my feminine side. Sentimentality overwhelms me as I get older. Lately, the simplest, corniest things can bring tears: love songs from Rodgers and Hammerstein musicals, "If I Loved You" from Carousel, and "Heather On the Hill" from Brigadoon. They remind me both of my childhood and past love affairs. To me, that's sentimental, that's vulnerable, that's feminine.

Being a nightclub proprietress was wonderful and the club was hot but doing it right cost a lot. After three months I had to choose between doing it on a smaller budget or not doing it, and I chose the latter. I still host evenings at the Paradise Lounge sometimes. I occasionally perform around town, at clubs, the Castro Street Fair, wherever. I've got two different acts: strict cabaret, Goddess and Piano, concentrating on high class Broadway stuff from the '30s and '60s. My second act is psychedelic acoustic folk rock incorporating original songs, and groovy old classics from Van Morrison and Stevie Nicks.

Singing is wonderful, but I will never completely abandon the stage. I'm too theater damaged. My fantasy is the lead role in the original 1920s *LuLu*. Maybe a Kathy Acker-style version of it, sort of a pornographic punk version with a chorus of boys behind me singing really loud, like in *Applause*. That's what I was born to do. I love a real theater with dressing rooms and the knocking, "Five minutes, Miss Brice." That atmosphere. It's a Bernadette Peters problem. I'm shameless at this point; I'll come right out and say it.

I'm that queer. I could play Mama Rose in *Gypsy*, Fanny Brice in *Funny Girl*, or maybe I should just star in *The Unsinkable Bambi Lake*, because the old tragic myths from Tennessee Williams, Jean Genet, and Hubert Selby Jr., will no longer do.

Afterword

What can I say about the trans movement these days, twenty years later? Well, Laverne Cox of *Orange is the New Black* is on the cover of *Time* magazine – she's the brother of Reginald Cox who was a local San Francisco diva in the '90s. RuPaul's *Drag Race* has created starlets every season and they go out on tour, there's a circuit.

There has become a difference between gay boys dressing up doing hilarious routines and transgenders who are more earnest; they aren't trannies, in fact they got Trannyshack to change its name.

The person who really made a difference with the term "transgender" is Kate Bornstein, and she has had a real impact. Her book sold; she was on *Donahue* years ago. She made a very strong distinction that there was a real difference between gender and sexuality, and she brought that message to America. She broke through and all of a sudden there were Gender Studies being taught at universities and everywhere. It all goes back to Kate. She was a man at Brown University and she was clear, saying, "I'm not a transsexual." She is attracted to women. She's a transgender lesbian.

The group that's moving forward, they're different than the boys who like to dress up on weekends. Years ago, when I started in Germany with Romy in '76, I walked in and saw her. She was living as a woman and running a drag club. In those days, it was more a prostitution scene for survival. You'd be like, "I'm not going to get a job at Macy's so how will I make it?" It's unfortunate but that's the way America dealt with it. I eventually slid toward that when I got back from Berlin. That's how a lot of people were able to afford a sex change; it's tens of thousands of dollars.

I've aged out of that at 66, living in fabulous subsidized senior housing, and getting SSI. It's great. Seriously, I live in a new building and most of my neighbors are elderly Asians; it's quiet, no drama. I was an angry messed-up person for so long, years, but that's in the past. I wonder why I was so angry for so long… it must have been because I didn't fit in anywhere. I was scared; I wasn't able to find a permanent partner. I'm calm now but it took an awful long time for me. Things happen when you get quasi-famous.

Silas Howard's short film about me played at film festivals. He had a great cinematographer. That was the last time I was really glammed up. I don't want to engage with people on the street in that way any more, I prefer to be low-key these days. My breasts are gone; I had them for 30 years. One was leaking so it was time to get them removed. RuPaul rarely appears in drag anymore. He dresses as a man. He never identified as transgender.

Justin Vivian Bond doing "The Golden Age of Hustlers" has been great. Silas did a great job with that video. When I wrote that song, all the Mabuhay people I hung out with were ten years younger than me. After the clubs closed for the night, where was I supposed to go? I'd go to Polk Street. "The Golden Age of Hustlers" is a romanticized version of what went on. It's about needing a place to stay.

What's going on with my musical act? We used to play at Chicken John's bar in the Mission, The Odeon, that was a scene. It's the only bar I've ever been in where you could literally dance on the bar. They had variety acts and that was perfect for us. Our act has about thirty of the old songs. People really appreciated it because no one else was doing it. We last performed a while ago in a space in Hayes Valley.

All through the last twenty years, no matter what, I have always had Birdie, my piano player. Birdie-Bob Watt.

Acknowledgments

The author wishes to thank the following individuals, without whom this book would not exist:

Alvin Orloff; Birdie-Bob Watt; Jennifer Blowdryer; Sue Brisk; Exene Cervenka; David Colone; Ginger Coyote; Heidi; Jennifer Joseph; Scott Idleman; Veronica Klaus; Daniel Nicoletta; Brad Noble; Bucky Sinister; Julie Stein; Kent Taylor; Gwyn Waters; Lenore Waters; Danielle Willis; Justin Vivian Bond; and Silas Howard.

All photographs are from the collection of Bambi Lake. The photographs in this book are produced with grateful thanks to the following photographers: Daniel Nicoletta; Frances Purcell; Sue Brisk; Alexander Fazekas- Paul; Kent Taylor; Julie Stein; Ric Warren; Heidi; Bradley Noble; Billy Bowers; and Ana Grillo.

Every effort has been made to locate all copyright holders for the photographs used. We would be pleased to hear from any copyright holder who has not been contacted.

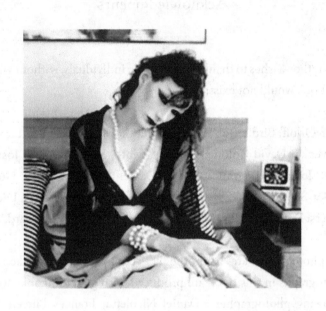

Silas Howard & Bambi